Speech Coursebook

3rd Edition

Karrin Anderson

Final Exam
Wed May 9th   Room!
3:40 - 5:40
      Bring Blue Book

THOMSON

Australia · Canada · Mexico · Singapore · Spain · United Kingdom · United States

Speech Coursebook
Karrin Anderson

Custom Editor:
Danielle Walsh

Project Development Editor:
Lea Riddle

Marketing Coordinators:
Lindsay Annett and Sara Mercurio

Production/Manufacturing Supervisor:
Donna M. Brown

Project Coordinator:
Rebecca Walker

Pre-Media Services Supervisor:
Dan Plofchan

Rights and Permissions Specialist:
Kalina Hintz

Senior Prepress Specialist:
Kim Fry

Cover Design:
Krista Pierson

Printer:
Globus

For permission to use material from this text or product, contact us by:
Tel (800) 730-2214
Fax (800) 730 2215
www.thomsonrights.com

Speech Coursebook / Karrin Anderson –
3 rd Edition
p. 150
ISBN 0-759-36365-X

Acknowledgments

The production of this *Coursebook* was a collaborative effort. I wish to thank present and past members of the SPCC 200 teaching staff for their outstanding contributions. This book could not have been completed without their encouragement, criticism, and creativity. In particular, I wish to acknowledge the work done by my predecessors, Dr. David L. Vancil, Dr. Sue D. Pendell, and Dr. Carl R. Burgchardt who developed the concept of a *Speech Coursebook* into its present form. The Lecturers and Teaching Assistants for SPCC 200 generated many of the listening, critique, and work sheets. It has been a pleasure to work with Danielle Walsh, David Hall, and others at Thomson Wadsworth. I am grateful to the following individuals, who granted me permission to print their original work: Melissa Ritter, Naomi Lederer, Jennifer Bone, T.M. Linda Scholz, Kirsten Pullen, Josh Heuman, AnnaMarie Adams Mann, and Carl Burgchardt. Finally, I wish to thank the former students of SPCC 200 who agreed to publish their outlines or speech manuscripts in this *Coursebook*: Katherine Gould, Katelyn Briggs, Nathan Frasier, and Julie Kreps.

TABLE OF CONTENTS

COURSE POLICIES AND INFORMATION
Student information sheet   1
Midterm course evaluation   3
Public Speaking Skills: Prepping for Personal, Academic, and Professional Success   5
Course policies   6

UNIT ONE: INTRODUCTION TO SPEAKING
Diagnostic speech assignment   11
Organizing your first speech   12
Why it's important: index cards   12
Critique sheets   13
Self-evaluation sheet   17

UNIT TWO: NARRATIVE SPEAKING
Tell a story speech assignment   19
Why it's important: time management   20
Choosing a story topic   20
Sample tell a story speech: "When Did You Say Your Birthday Was?"   21
Topic proposal   25
Critique sheets   27
Listening sheets   31
Self-evaluation sheet   37

UNIT THREE: INFORMATIVE SPEAKING
Informative speech assignment   39
Choosing a topic for your informative speech   40
Why it's important: complete sentence outlining   40
Research at Colorado State University   41
Creating the works cited page   44
Audience survey worksheet   47
PowerPoint Workshop   49
Pitfalls of PowerPoint   51
Sample informative speech outline: "Little Schoolhouse on the Prairie"   53
Topic proposal   59
Critique sheets   61
Listening sheets   65
Self-evaluation sheet   75

UNIT FOUR: INVITATIONAL SPEAKING
Invitational dialogue assignment   77
Why it's important: appreciating multiple perspectives   78
Invitational dialogue feedback sheets   79

UNIT FIVE: PERSUASIVE SPEAKING
Policy speech assignment 87
Why it's important: learning to advocate for change 88
The argument triangle 88
Advocating for a policy: Need, Plan, and Practicality 89
Fielding questions after a persuasive speech 91
Sample policy speech outline: "Solving Our Nitrate Problem" 93
Sample policy speech outline: "Compact Florescent Light Bulbs" 98
Topic proposal 103
Audience survey 105
Policy speech worksheet 107
Critique sheets 111
Listening sheets 115
Self-evaluation sheet 123

UNIT SIX: COMMEMORATIVE SPEAKING
Commemorative speech assignment 125
Preparing your commemorative speech 126
Sample commemorative speech manuscript: "Lina" 132
Topic proposal 135
Critique sheets 137
Listening sheets 141
Self-evaluation sheet 147

Midterm Course Evaluation

Semester and Year: _____

Instructor's Name: _____

In the Department of Speech Communication at Colorado State University, we believe that Communication courses are about empowerment. Broadly, we hope to equip students with the skills they need for democratic citizenship. We also want students to walk out of class each day with a greater understanding of their choices and options as communicators and with an increased sense of control over their communication behavior. We can only achieve these goals if you are an active participant in the course. Take a moment to reflect upon what's working and what's not in this class. Consider not only your instructor's strengths and course design, but also your own contributions to class.

What do you feel are the strengths of this class? (consider things like interaction with your instructor, teaching styles, use of class time, clarity of instructor expectations, textbook and coursebook material, speaking assignments and activities, etc.)

What, in your opinion, could be changed or improved upon?

Regarding your preceding answer, suggest specific revisions to the course that would fulfill existing course standards and goals:

What, if anything, could you do personally to improve your experience in this course? (i.e., improve attendance or participation, complete the reading in a more timely fashion, allow more time to prepare speeches, etc.)

Public Speaking Skills: Prepping for Personal, Academic, and Professional Success[1]

Welcome to SPCC 200! Chances are, you're here because your major requires you to be here. That's okay. We understand that speaking in public is a daunting prospect—one that most people would avoid if they could. We also know that you won't be able to avoid it forever, and learning the principles of public speaking will benefit you in many different situations, not just the ones where you find yourself behind a podium. A great deal of research has been done on the benefits of public speaking skills. Researchers have found that:

Communication skills benefit you in your personal life.
In this class, you will learn to be a confident speaker, an attentive listener, and a well-rounded and informed individual.
- Students who complete courses in public speaking *feel more confident* about themselves.[2]
- Communication skills *enhance your relationships* with other people.[3]
- One must understand communication dynamics to *build a successful family.*[4]

Communication skills help you succeed academically.
In this class, you will practice academic skills such as writing, research, outlining, logic and argumentation, and creative language use.
- Communication education *improves critical thinking skills.*[5]

Communication skills promote professional success.
In this class, you will learn how to adapt your message to diverse audiences, speak with polish and conviction, and present your ideas in a concrete, organized, and persuasive manner.
- Employers report that *communication skills rank high* among the most important job-related skills they want their employees to have.[6]
- Job-seeking experts advise students to *hone their oral and written communication* skills before they enter the job market.[7]
- Employers predict that *increased communication skills will be needed* for jobs in the 21st century, and although 90% of responding employers said that communication skills are essential for success, they also indicated that many applicants lack effective communication skills in job interviews.[8]

---

[1] Morreale, S.P., Osborn, M. M., & Pearson, J.C. (2000). Why communication is Important: A Rationale for the Centrality of the Study of Communication. Journal of the Association for Communication Administration, 29, 1-25.
[2] Ford, W.S. Z., & Wolvin, A.D. (1993). The differential impact of a basic communication course on perceived communication competencies in class, work, and social contexts. Communication Education, 42, 215-233.
[3] Backlund, P. (1989). What should be the role of speech communication in the general education of students? In The Future of Communication Education. Annandale, VA: NCA.
[4] Pearson, J.C. & Sessler, C.J. (1991, May). Family communication and health: Maintaining marital satisfaction and quality of life. Paper presented at the Annual Meeting of the International Communication Association, Chicago, IL. (ERIC Document Reproduction Service No. ED335722).
[5] Allen, M. & Berkowitz, S. Hunt, S. & Louden, A. (1999). A meta-analysis of the impact of forensics and communication education on critical thinking. Communication Education, 48, 18-30.
[6] Kim, Y. & Wright, C.E. (1989). A study of general education requirements in vocational education programs. Menlo Park, CA: Educational Evaluation and Research, Inc. (ERIC Document Reproduction Service No. ED 312482).
[7] Bardwell, C.B. (1997). Standing out in the crowd. Black Collegian, 28, 71-79.
[8] Peterson, M.S. (1997). Personnel interviewers' perceptions of the importance and adequacy of applicants' communication skills. Communication Education, 46, 287-291.

COURSE POLICIES

Attendance

The credits you earn in this class are based on participation as well as performance. The learning experience is not confined to exams you take and speeches you give. A public speaking course involves not just speaking, but also listening, critique, feedback, and facilitation. In addition, speakers need an audience on performance days. Consequently, regular attendance and participation is required. Because illnesses and emergencies do arise during the course of the semester, one week's worth of absences are allowed without penalty:

Fall/Spring Semester
50 minute class: 3 unpenalized absences
75 minute class: 2 unpenalized absences

Summer 4-week session: 1 unpenalized absence
Summer 8-week session 2 unpenalized absences

Provided it is not a performance or exam day, no explanation is required for the missed day, however the student is responsible for obtaining any lecture material, handouts, or announcements covered in class. These absences should be reserved for illness, emergencies, family engagements, and participation in university-sponsored activities. **After your unpenalized absences have been used, each unexcused absence will result in a *15 point per absence deduction* from your final grade (30 points during the 4-week Summer sessions)**. If your social, academic, extra-curricular, or employment schedule will interfere with attendance and participation in SPCC 200, please consider taking this course a different semester.

Speech days: You must attend class on days you are scheduled to give a speech. Failure to give your speech on the assigned day or to provide a replacement from your class will result in the grade of "zero" for that assignment.

Excused absences: Occasionally, a student may miss a speech or have an extra absence for which they may not be penalized. There are five standards by which we determine if an absence is excused. Before asking your instructor for an exemption, however, be certain that your situation conforms to *every one* of the following criteria:

1. The absence must be unexpected. There was no way you could prepare for it or plan ahead.
2. The circumstances of your absence must be beyond your control.
3. The nature of your excuse must be serious: a death or medical crisis in your immediate family; onset of an incapacitating illness; or a severe accident.
4. If you are physically able, you *must* contact your instructor or leave a message *prior* to the time you are expected to give a speech or complete an assignment.
5. You must be able to document your excuse in writing.

University activities: If you will miss class due to participation in university-sponsored sports or activities, please discuss your schedule with your instructor *early* in the semester. Provide a letter, signed by a coach or sponsor, verifying your participation in the activity. Absences for events will count as unpenalized absences (you may not miss 3 classes for activities and then get additional free absences on top of that), but if you have more than 3 activity-related absences those can be excused if advance notice and documentation is provided. Please make every effort to schedule your speeches on days that do not conflict with your travel schedule. If your activity requires you to miss more than 4 classes during the course of the semester, please take SPCC 200 a different semester.

<u>Tardiness</u>: Tardiness is particularly disruptive in a public speaking class. <u>Never</u> walk in on another student who is giving a speech. Wait at the door until their speech is concluded. Additionally, it is important to come to class on time so that your instructor can make an accurate record of your attendance. If you come to class late, after attendance has been taken, you are *personally responsible* for informing the instructor that you were present. Habitual tardiness may result in the loss of attendance points.

<u>Cell phones</u>: Cell phones are particularly disruptive in a public speaking class. Please turn your phone off prior to entering class. If your cell phone is a continual disruption, your instructor will assess an appropriate penalty.

Computer/Technology Problems

Computer malfunctions do not constitute an "excuse" or an "emergency." Prepare your assignments far enough in advance so that when your computer malfunctions (*and it will*) you will be able to rectify the problem and turn in the assignment on time. Allow for printer, disk, server, service provider, and other technology problems. Also, have a back-up plan in case classroom technology fails during your speech. You will be expected to go on with the presentation, just as you would if you encountered a technology problem on the job.

Academic Integrity

Students in SPCC 200 are expected to do their own work. Research, visual aids, and outlines for speeches must be products of a student's individual, original work. You may not work with students in your own or other sections of SPCC 200 on the same speech topic, and any information you obtain from outside sources for use in your speech must be cited orally in the speech and credited in the bibliography. Failure to conform to Colorado State University's standards for academic integrity can result in failure of the assignment, failure of the course, and/or reporting of the student's conduct to the university's Conflict Resolution and Student Conduct Service office. For a detailed explanation of CSU's academic integrity guidelines, see the *General Catalog*.

Accommodating Special Needs

Students who require special accommodations during testing or instruction should first contact Resources for Disabled Students, 100 General Services, Fort Collins, CO 80523, (970) 491-6385 (V/TDD). Information about Resources for Disabled Students can be found online at http://www.colostate.edu/Depts/RDS/. The SPCC 200 staff is happy to accommodate the specific needs of our students, provided the policies and procedures outlined by Resources for Disabled Students are followed. Please discuss your needs with your instructor <u>at the beginning of the semester</u> so that the requisite accommodations may be put in place. Be advised that speech deadlines are firm. A last-minute extension will not be granted.

Grading Standards

Although each assignment has a distinct set of grading criteria, there are general standards that can be applied to all of the speeches:

The "B" or "A" speech presents a thesis that is significantly challenging for college students. The analysis reflects superior understanding of the subject and its appropriate development. The central idea is introduced so as to engage the concern as well as the interest of the listener. The organization of main points and supporting materials is strikingly clear. The delivery of the speech is marked by excellent choice of language, articulation, and animation. The speech reflects a high degree of polish as presented in final form. While a "B" speech is above average, an "A" speech is clearly superior in all areas.

The "C" speech meets the basic requirements of the assignment. It develops a clearly defined idea that is phrased and presented in a manner significant for the audience. There is supporting material for the main points. The speech has a recognizable developmental pattern. The speaker makes adequate use of basic physical and vocal delivery. The "C" speech is an average speech.

The "D" or "F" speech treats a topic in a trite or inconsequential way, or it may not conform to the assignment. The thesis may be vague or too broad to cover in the allocated time. There is a lack of structure and often a considerable amount of irrelevant, superficial material. There is little attempt to adapt to the audience and situation. Delivery is broken or lacks variety, and there may be problems with the choice of language. While the "D" speech is below average, it does have some saving grace. The "F" speech has none.

You should understand assignment criteria and your instructor's expectations before you prepare each speech. If you are unclear about assignment specifications, visit with your instructor about your questions and concerns. If you do not understand why you received a particular grade on a speech, schedule an appointment to talk with your instructor. Our goal is to help you become the best speaker you can be. That goal can only be accomplished if 1) the instructor evaluates your work frankly and accurately, and 2) you and your instructor work together to improve your performance. If you discuss problems and concerns with your instructor early in the semester (rather than two weeks before the end of the semester) the chances are greatly improved that this class will be a productive and positive experience for you.

Improvement

As you may have noticed, the speeches are worth increasingly more as the semester progresses. This provides a built-in reward for improvement. As you learn more, gain experience, and become more comfortable speaking in front of audiences, your performance should improve. As this occurs, the speeches become worth more. Thus, mistakes that are made early in the semester are not as costly as mistakes made later. The one exception to this is the Commemorative Speech, which, because of its short length and manuscript style of delivery, is not worth as much as the other speeches.

Naturally, as the course progresses, your instructor's expectations regarding your speaking ability will increase, too. As you complete each unit of study, you should continue to use the information and insights gained from previous units. Even if your grades on speeches remain the same, you actually are improving because you must master additional principles with each speech. If you did not progress over the course of the semester, your grades would go down. Of course, we all hope that, by the end of the semester, you are pleased with your performance and satisfied with your final grade. We should stress, however, that you will be evaluated by the excellence of your work alone. Effort, *per se*, is not a factor in grading.

Grading Scale

Below is the point distribution and corresponding letter grade for each assignment in class:

Letter Grade	Tell a Story	Inform-ative	Invitational	Policy	Commem-orative	Quizzes	Final Exam	Misc. (homework, participation activities)
A+	50	200	50	250	100	100	150	100
A	48	192	48	240	96	96	144	96
A-	46	186	46	233	93	93	140	93
B+	44	178	44	223	89	89	134	89
B	43	172	43	215	86	86	129	86
B-	41	166	41	208	83	83	125	83
C+	39	158	39	198	79	79	119	79
C	38	152	38	190	76	76	114	76
C-	36	146	36	183	73	73	110	73
D+	34	138	34	173	69	69	104	69
D	33	132	33	165	66	66	99	66
D-	31	126	31	158	63	63	95	63
F	29 and below	118 and below	29 and below	148 and below	59 and below	59 and below	89 and below	59 and below

Here is the 1000-point scale we will use to assign final course grades:

1000-933	A	799-767	C+
932-900	A-	766-733	C
899-867	B+	732-700	C-
866-833	B	699-600	D
832-800	B-	599 and below	F

Grade Record

This sheet can serve as a record of the due dates for each major assignment and grades you earn throughout the semester. Fill in the *number of points* you earn as you complete each assignment.

Diagnostic: Date _____ Grade <u>Pass/Fail</u>

Tell a Story: Date _____ Grade _____

Informative: Date _____ Grade _____

Invitational: Date _____ Grade _____

Policy: Date _____ Grade _____

Commemorative: Date _____ Grade _____

Homework, Etc. :

                Grade _____

Quizzes:

                Grade _____

Final Exam: Date _____ Grade _____

TOTAL POINTS: _____

To determine your overall grade, compare the points you have earned with the grading scale on the previous page. During the semester, you can add the points you have earned and divide it by the total points possible for the assignments completed.

UNIT ONE: INTRODUCTION TO SPEAKING

📄 **Reading:** *Invitation to Public Speaking*, Ch. 1-3

Unit Objectives: Upon completion of this unit, you should understand:

✓ the power and influence of public speaking

✓ the public speaking process

✓ when and why we speak in public

✓ overcoming nervousness in public speaking

✓ the connection between listening and creating community

✓ why we sometimes fail to listen

✓ how to listen effectively and ethically

Assignment: Diagnostic Speech

Prepare and present a 2-3 minute speech on a topic specified by your instructor. This speech is designed to "diagnose" your speaking strengths and areas that need improvement. It will be graded on a pass/fail basis. If you attempt to complete the assignment in good faith, you will pass.

The Diagnostic Speech Assignment Emphasizes the Following Skills:

⇨ Organization: Make sure your speech has an identifiable introduction, body, and conclusion.

⇨ Extemporaneous Delivery: Engage your audience with a dynamic speaking style and sustained eye contact. Deliver the speech from a "bare bones" outline on index cards.

⇨ Time Management: Practice your speech so that you conform to the time limit. This is probably the most important rule. If several students take more than 3 minutes, there will not be enough class time for everyone to speak.

☑ Tips & Suggestions: Organizing Your First Speech

Even a short speech should follow sound organizational principles. Make sure your diagnostic speech has an identifiable introduction, body, and conclusion. Use each section of the speech to accomplish the following specific goals.

Introduction
- Attention-Getter: Begin by gaining the audience's attention and getting them interested in your topic. Start with a short story, an interesting question, a unique fact—something that will grab audience members and compel them to listen to you.
- Thesis & Preview: Reveal your speech topic, the purpose of your speech, and preview your main points.

Body
- Organize the body of your speech into distinct main points. Don't just lump all the information together. Divide it according to topics and make choices about what you should include and what you should leave out of the speech.

Conclusion
- Review: Briefly summarize the main points you covered in the speech.
- "When to Clap" line: Audiences need a signal that the speech has ended and they can clap. Plan a specific closing line for your speech that lets your audience know, definitively, that you're done. Try to make it more creative than "Thank you," "That's all," or "I'm done."

Good organization enhances your credibility, makes your speeches clear and interesting, and helps you accomplishing your communication goals. Start practicing the basics of organization now.

Why It's Important: Index Cards

Putting your speaking notes on index cards rather than sheets of paper helps improve your delivery in a number of ways:

- Key words and phrases fit on an index card, but your whole speech won't. Index cards help you create good speaker's notes.

- Since index cards are small and sturdy you can hold them and still move away from the podium a bit to incorporate movement into your speech. Remember, in many speaking situations, you will not have a lectern to stand behind or a podium to put your notes on!

Tip: Number your index cards so that you can easily verify they are complete and in the correct order. Cards can get mixed up or dropped if you're not careful.

Critique Sheet: Diagnostic Speech

+	Excellent
✓	Satisfactory
--	Needs improvement
0	Failed to complete

Name _____

INTRODUCTION

Captured audience attention _____

Previewed main points _____

BODY

Main points clear _____

CONCLUSION

Signaled start of conclusion _____

Reviewed main points _____

Decisive/artistic last line _____

DELIVERY

Maintained eye contact _____

Used vocal variety _____

Projected adequately _____

Pronunciation correct _____

Articulation clear _____

Rate appropriate _____

Paused effectively _____

Gestures purposeful _____

Mannerisms appropriate _____

Facial expression _____

Extemporaneous style _____

Effective speaking notes _____

OVERALL EVALUATION

Completed in time limit _____

Topic appropriate _____

Specific strengths and areas for improvement:

Instructor comments and suggestions:

TIME _____

GRADE: Pass Fail

Self-Evaluation Sheet: Diagnostic Speech

Name:_____Topic:_____

1. After viewing your video, identify your speaking strengths and weaknesses as they appeared in your Diagnostic Speech.

2. Specifically, what would you like to improve about your speech-related skills throughout the semester?

3. What will you need to do differently for your next speech in this class, in terms of preparation and practice, to improve your performance?

4. What are some of the fears you have related to public speaking?

5. What do you hope to take from this class to use in your future communication experiences?

UNIT TWO: NARRATIVE SPEAKING

📄 **Reading:** *Invitation to Public Speaking*, Ch. 5, 7 (section on Narratives), 12, 13

Unit Objectives: Upon completion of this unit, you should be able to:

✓ Adapt your topic to your class community

✓ Use narrative to connect with your audience

✓ Understand the power of language

✓ Use language that is memorable and pleasing

✓ Engage the audience with your delivery

Assignment: Tell a Story Speech

Tell a story that includes a constructive insight, moral, or theme. The story can be from your own life or can be about someone or something else. The story can be dramatic, humorous, inspiring, suspenseful, or poignant. Whatever approach you choose, your story should be sincere, appropriate for the classroom environment, written in your own words, and designed to help you connect with audience members. The speech should be 4-5 minutes in length and should be delivered extemporaneously. Prior to the delivery of the speech, submit 2 copies of a typed, double-spaced manuscript of your speech in paragraph form. Avoid spelling, typographical, or grammatical errors.

The Tell a Story Speech Assignment Emphasizes the Following Skills:

⇨ Organization: This speech differs from the others this semester in that it will not have a traditional introduction, body, and conclusion. However, you will need to think carefully about your speech's organization. Order the information in your narrative so that it will draw in your audience and unfold in a compelling way.

⇨ Language Use: The best storytellers choose their words carefully and employ stylistic devices to enliven their narratives. Plan and practice your language use.

⇨ Delivery: Nothing ruins a good story faster than poor delivery. Narrative speaking requires confidence, timing, and conviction—each of those require practice. Use polished extemporaneous speaking style. You should <u>not</u> read this speech word-for-word from notes, but you should practice it enough so that your language use is fluid and consistent. Also work on having sustained eye contact with individual audience members, try to identify and eliminate distracting nonverbal behaviors, and use vocal variety and projection to add dynamism to the performance.

⇨ Time management: Mediocre stories ramble. The best storytellers have the ability to convey emotion and rich description in a relatively short amount of time. Make sure your story does not exceed 5 minutes.

Why It's Important: Time Management   By Melissa Ritter

Time is an important factor in today's society. We are all faced with time constraints every day. We expect movies to begin on time and friends to meet us at a specified time. Newscasters have an allotted amount of time to cover a story before a station must move to a commercial or another story. In order to ensure enough time to cover all of the issues in a meeting, business people must conform to a specific agenda. As a student, you rely on your professors to adjourn class on time so that you can make it to your next class promptly. When an event runs overtime or when a person is late, people become agitated, and rightfully so. Our world is regulated by the clock.

Like the rest of society, you too have time constraints in your public speaking class. Each type of speech that is given in your class will have different minimum and maximum time limits. Although you may not think so now, you will soon discover that it is usually quite easy to exceed the minimum time limits for a speech. On the other hand, staying within the maximum time for a speech may require special effort, such as close editing and repeated practice.

These time limits must be respected because some of your classmates will need to present their speeches on the same day you are giving yours. If one person goes overtime on a speech, it affects the next presentation. This is not fair to your classmates, and it isn't good preparation for the standards of timeliness you will face after graduation.

Conforming to the time limits is also a significant factor in determining your speech grade. Severe violations of time limits will result in grade penalties. In order to avoid this unpleasant consequence, keep your speech tightly focused, limit the amount of information you intend to cover, follow a clear structure, and *practice, practice, practice*.

☑ **Tips & Suggestions: Choosing a Story Topic**

Before you settle on a speech topic, think about what makes for a good story. Stories can engage audiences in many different ways. They can tap into common human experiences; they can invoke emotions; they can unfold in clever or surprising ways; they can be beautifully told; they can inspire, entertain, or even frighten.

Next, think about your strengths and weaknesses as a speaker. You may want to tell a really funny story, but if you lack timing, don't project particularly well, and have mediocre eye contact it will be tough to get your audience to laugh. Choose a story theme that complements your speaking style.

After you have assessed your speaking strengths and thought about the types of reactions you'd like to evoke in your audience, think back on your life experiences. What stories stand out to you, personally? What anecdotes offer the most potential for artistry, emotion, and audience engagement? As a general rule, it's a good idea to choose a topic/story that you *know* and *love*. If you feel passionate about your topic, you are less likely to be nervous during the speech and more likely to hold the audience's attention.

Sample Tell a Story Speech
for analysis and discussion

SPCC 200, [section]
[Date]

"When Did You Say Your Birthday Was?"
by Nathan Frasier

We've all been there before. Maybe it was for college maybe it was for work but it's an occurrence we all share. It's that first time we experience freedom from our parents. For me it came with my freshman year of college. I was on top of the world, knew it all, and nothing was going to stop me. Long-term plans were not important; it was time to live in the moment. Unfortunately, that feeling of freshman immortality can come crashing down with the simple words of "When did you say your birthday was?"

It was February and I was about to leave the hills of Tennessee for a vacation in the mountains of Colorado. The trip was a gift from my parents that I was very grateful for since I could never afford it myself. The plan was for a high school buddy, Joe, and me to fly out and meet another friend, Lindsey who went to school at CSU. The highlight of the trip: skiing!

A few of Lindsey's friends from the dorm heard we wanted to go skiing and mentioned we could use their passes and save a few bucks. They said they let other people borrow them all the time. Being a poor college student I thought it was a great idea--maybe I would be able to eat something other than Top Raman with the money I saved. Joe had other thoughts on the matter and expressed his hesitancy about the idea. Joe has always been one to worry so I poked fun at him and blew it off.

The next day we were up before the sun and headed for the mountains, the weather looked great--blue sky and sunshine. I was flying high with excitement. Feeling energized, happy, and, of course, filled with a strong dose of freshman immortality I unloaded our equipment and we headed for the lift. I went strutting down the line, wanting to fit in with all the real skiers. Nothing could stop me. Nothing except those words, "When did you say your birthday was?" Blindsided. The air was knocked from my lungs, and my knees began to shake, threatening to give out at any second. Of course I knew when my birthday was, but my name was not on that pass. I WAS BUSTED! My mind whirled with ideas and excuses but my mouth wouldn't move and neither would my legs which I desperately tried to coax to run very fast the other way. I was suddenly in a movie, put on slow motion; time seemed to stop. A few more stabs at the right date failed. 1 in 365 aren't very good odds.

The guy who scanned my pass asked me to follow him, ripping me from my support group of friends, and turned me over to his supervisor. The supervisor escorted me to a room, behind a door that read "Authorized Personnel Only." Guessing I was not authorized personnel I had a sinking feeling life was going to get worse. The guy left me in the room for a few minutes, and once again I was in the movies--the scene where they question the accused, letting them sit in that small room with the two way mirror, sweating. I was definitely sweating. My mouth was dry and I wanted to be buried in a hole. My thoughts filled with Joe's cautions the night before. The old saying "what goes around comes around" did not sound trite at that moment. I had made fun of him for not wanting to take the passes and now I sat in a room I didn't belong in.

The supervisor returned and to my relief was very nice but straightforward. He didn't yell or threaten me but he made it very clear this was a serious matter and there were consequences to be paid. Those consequences were that I lost the pass, had to pay for a half-day pass, a "lesson learner" as he called it, and to buy a full day pass if I wanted to ski that day. He was also sure to stress the point that I had gotten off easy, something about calling the police and pressing charges. The burden was lifted slightly but my mind was occupied with the amount of money I was about to depart with. A half-day pass: $38, a full day pass: $61, payment to the kid I borrowed the pass from $200, and no, there was nothing priceless about it. I became an even poorer college kid and was knocked off the top of the world.

I did end up skiing that day and had some fun, though not as much fun as I could have had. Actually, I don't really remember the skiing very well but I have always remembered the lesson I learned and being an expensive one it hit home a little harder. There are sayings for these times in life, "what goes around comes around," "pay a little now or a lot later," "honesty is the best policy," and I'm sure you can think of a few of your own. They seem silly, almost useless, but remember that behind each of those sayings is a story. My story brought my freshman ego back to earth very quickly. Next time you're faced with a choice to cut a corner, I hope it saves you a few dollars. Remember, there are more exciting things you can spend money on than life lessons.

Topic Proposal: Tell a Story Speech

Name:_____

Propose two potential topics for your Tell a Story Speech. List them below, in order of preference, and explain why you think your story ideas would be compelling to your audience.

Topic 1:

Briefly explain what your story will be about:

What specific strategies will you use to make this story compelling for your audience?

What will be your story's constructive insight, moral, or theme?

Topic 2:

Briefly explain what your story will be about:

What specific strategies will you use to make this story compelling for your audience?

What will be your story's constructive insight, moral, or theme?

Instructor Comments:

Topic 1 _____Approved _____Not Approved

Topic 2 _____Approved _____Not Approved

Listening Sheet: Tell a Story Speech
Delivery

Listener:

Speaker: Topic:

Identify 2 of the speaker's delivery *strengths* (comment on volume, pitch, rate, pauses, vocal variety, pronunciation, articulation, dialect, appearance, bodily action, gestures, and eye contact).

Identify 2 *areas for improvement* in the speaker's delivery (comment on volume, pitch, rate, pauses, vocal variety, pronunciation, articulation, dialect, appearance, bodily action, gestures, and eye contact).

What speech preparation or practice techniques would you recommend to the speaker to improve her/his delivery?

Listening Sheet: Tell a Story Speech
Audience Adaptation

Listener:

Speaker: Topic:

What made this speech most compelling for you, as a member of the audience?

Was there anything about this speech that detracted from its audience appeal? Explain how the speaker might have been more effective.

What audience adaptation strategies do you think you will try in future speeches, based on what you've seen during the Tell a Story round?

Listening Sheet: Tell a Story Speech
Language

Listener:

Speaker: Topic:

Identify specific lines from the speech that used language in a particularly memorable or compelling way.

What could the speaker have done to make his/her language use more effective?

Evaluate the relationship between language use and delivery in this speech.

Self-Evaluation Sheet: Tell a Story Speech

Name:_____Topic:_____

1. How did the audience react to your story? Did their reactions surprise you? Why or why not?

2. What did you learn from this speech that will enable you to engage audiences effectively in future speeches?

3. After reviewing your video, evaluate the quality of your delivery (extemporaneous style, eye contact, gestures, bodily action, facial expression, projection, vocalized pauses, vocal variety, etc.). Identify two strengths and two areas for improvement in your delivery.

UNIT THREE: INFORMATIVE SPEAKING

📄 **Reading:** *Invitation to Public Speaking*, Ch. 4, 6, 7, 9-11, 14-15

Unit Objectives: Upon completion of this unit, you should understand:

✓ how to select a topic and purpose

✓ guidelines and organizational principles of informative speaking

✓ how to begin and end your speech

✓ the different types of outlines and how to prepare them

✓ how to incorporate quality supporting materials into your speech

✓ how to design and use visual aids

Assignment: Informative Speech

Prepare and present a 4-6 minute speech that conveys useful or interesting information to an audience. Cite at least 4-6 different <u>sources</u> for your audience during the speech (underline or highlight them on your outline), and include a minimum of one visual aid prepared specifically for this assignment. Prior to the delivery of the speech, submit 2 copies of a typed complete-sentence outline, including a works cited page. Avoid spelling, typographical, or grammatical errors.

The Informative Speech Assignment Emphasizes the Following Skills:

⇨ Organization: Focus on clarity in this speech. Your speech should have a well-developed introduction, distinct and logical main points, transitions between points, and a concise, compelling conclusion.

⇨ Research: This will be your first research-based speech of the semester. You should not only find credible sources and interesting supporting material, but you also must cite your sources clearly for the audience.

⇨ Outlining: A well-prepared complete-sentence outline will enable you to fulfill the organizational and research requirements of this assignment. Make sure you follow the outlining models in this *Coursebook* carefully.

⇨ Visual Support: This assignment allows you to practice two skills related to visual support: 1) preparing professional-quality visual aids, and 2) using them in a way that enhances (rather than detracts from) your credibility.

⇨ Speaker Credibility: Every aspect of your performance, from topic selection to research to delivery, should evidence your personal credibility as a speaker.

⇨ Audience Adaptation: Prepare your speech with your specific audience in mind. Devise strategies to give them useful information, keep them interested, and adapt to their knowledge of your topic.

☑ **Tips & Suggestions: Choosing a Topic For Your Informative Speech**

When you choose your topic for the Informative Speech, make sure it passes the *"Hmmm, that's interesting. I didn't know that" Test.* That's what you want your audience to be thinking after your speech. Many topics pass one part of the test, but your topic should pass both. For example, you could do a speech on how microprocessors function. Most people don't know much about that, but it's probably not an interesting speech either. Conversely, you might think that describing your favorite sport or hobby is interesting, but unless you find a truly unique angle, most people already know a lot about many popular sports and hobbies. So, while you should choose a topic to which you have a personal connection, you'll need to do research to find unique information that your audience is likely to find new and interesting.

Full Sentence Outline

I. Introduction
    A. Attention-getter
    B. Audience adaptation
    C. Credibility
    D. Thesis

Transition

II. Main point one
    A. Subpoint
      1) support

Why It's Important: Complete Sentence Outlining

The outline has several functions:

First, it *helps you prepare* your speech. Before we required complete sentence outlines, students would put off preparing for their speech, run out of time, and come to class unprepared. They would give disorganized, poorly researched, impromptu speeches. Grades actually improved after we instituted an outlining requirement because students were forced to develop main points and support each point with evidence in advance.

Second, the outline format *helps you organize* your speech. The reason you don't just write it in paragraph form is because we want you to think in terms of breaking your speech up into main points, supporting each point with evidence, having a distinct introduction and conclusion, and separating each point with connectives. The outline format helps you visualize the proper organization for a speech.

From a teaching perspective, the outline *helps your instructor to provide you with better feedback.* If a point is unclear in your speech, or a transition is poorly worded, they can respond specifically on your outline to what went wrong and how to improve it. If all they have is phrases on the outline, they cannot be as specific in their feedback and you're more likely to repeat the mistake on your next speech.

When you're preparing your complete sentence outline, refer to the models in this *Coursebook*. Be sure to include the <u>entire text</u> of your speech in outline form, label key introduction elements, transitions, and conclusion elements, underline or highlight your sources, and include 2 copies with a works cited page accompanying both.

☑ **Tips & Suggestions: Research at Colorado State University**   by Naomi Lederer

Researching a speech is like researching any other project. Read the suggestions found on the next few pages and make use of the Web pages referred to which recommend strategies and sources to use. Web pages created specifically for this course were designed in consultation with the Director of the SPCC 200 course, so you can use them with confidence.

Tips for Researching in the Library

1. ASK FOR HELP: There are service points in the library with staff to assist you. The primary location for research assistance is the Reference Desk.
2. PLAN AHEAD: Give yourself enough time—as in **hours**—to do your research. A speech researched in an hour or less is going to be noticeably lacking in depth and thoughtfulness. In addition, if you do your research just before a project is due, you won't have any time to *think* about the information you have found before you write it about it.
3. TOUR: Visit the library and get oriented to the layout and services of the building before you need to do research. There is a Virtual Tour you can also visit from any computer with access to the Web at <http://lib.colostate.edu/tour/>.

Choosing a Topic

Don't lock onto a topic until you know you can find enough—and the right kind—of information about it. You are doing current topics, and there is not going to be much information available for some subjects. By changing or adapting your topic near the beginning of your research, you don't waste time. Look for articles in the recommended indexes, and if you don't find at least five useful and available articles after looking through four or five indexes (don't give up after only one or two), CHANGE (or adapt) your topic!

A list of recommended indexes can be found at:
<http://lib.colostate.edu/howto/indexes.html>.
A number of these indexes, useful for current topics, have full text (complete articles) online.

Having difficulty choosing a topic? Look for suggestions on "Topic Selection Tips"
<http://lib.colostate.edu/howto/toptip.html>.

SPCC 200 Library Web Pages

The Web pages designed specifically for this course have useful information such as recommended reference books, Web pages, and indexes. The pages can be found at:
<http://lib.colostate.edu/research/speech/sp200.html>.

The page includes links to:

- Example Speeches   http://lib.colostate.edu/howto/expl.html
- Informative Speech   http://lib.colostate.edu/howto/inform.html
- Policy Speech (current topics)   http://lib.colostate.edu/howto/policy.html
- Commemorative Speech   http://lib.colostate.edu/howto/biog-r.html

Library Resources

A growing number of reference materials are available on the Web. However, there still are thousands of useful books in the reference collection, so don't overlook them!

- **General encyclopedias** are useful for background information.http://lib.colostate.edu/howto/genency.html has a list of general encyclopedias found in Morgan Library--scroll down to see the links to encyclopedias freely available on the Web.
- **Subject encyclopedias** are useful for specialized and more technical descriptions. See <http://lib.colostate.edu/howto/encyclo.html> for a list of recommended titles. They are listed by subject area; for example, societal, environment, and health.
- **Statistical sources** can provide valuable information that can support your argument. See a list of useful reference books with statistics at <http://lib.colostate.edu/howto/stats.html>.
- **Government documents** should not be overlooked. For unbiased research on contemporary topics, see *CQ Researcher* H 35 .E32 Reserve (latest year), Reference, and online through the databases page (and SPCC 200 Policy Speech page); *Congressional Quarterly Weekly Report* JK 1 .C5 Reference; and *Congressional Quarterly Almanac* JK 1 .C66 Reference.

You can identify books, government documents, books, microforms, journals, and more in the library catalog, SAGE. Check the status for availability. Write down the *call number* and the *location* for each item—then if you need directions, a staff member can assist you quickly.

How to Find Articles in Journals and Magazines

Finding articles is a five step process. Follow the steps in sequences, and, if necessary, ask for help at the Reference Desk.

Step 1: Select Indexes
> Use lists found on SPCC 200 Web pages or ask a reference librarian for suggestions.

Step 2: Search for the Topic
> Have different variations of terms in mind. You might call the topic "biodiversity," but if the index uses "diversity biology" you will miss relevant sources!

Step 3: Interpret the Information in the Index
> Identify the: Author, "Title of the Article." Journal/Magazine Title volume (date): and pages.

Step 4: Determine if the Libraries own the Journal. Details on how to do this are at <http://lib.colostate.edu/howto/owns.html>. Write down the call number and location (may vary by volume/year/issue) of the journal that the article is in.

Step 5: Locate the Journal and Find the Article in It.
> Is the journal in the Journal Room (journals shelved in call number order), on microfiche or microfilm, in the Moveable Shelves, in Storage, or even linked directly from the library catalog SAGE? You may need to request the article from Interlibrary Loan. Do your research as soon as possible so you have enough time to gather your materials!

If in Step 3 you discover that the article is full text online, you don't need to do steps 4 or 5—unless there are images or tables you wish to see that aren't shown. You will still need the article's bibliographical information for your bibliography or works cited list.

Evaluate Sources

It is critical that you evaluate the materials that you find. Inaccurate or misleading sources are useful to you as sources to criticize ONLY if you are aware that they are inaccurate and misleading! Use the evaluation tools listed below to help you determine *if* and *how* you want to use a resource.

How to Evaluate Books   http://lib.colostate.edu/howto/evalbk.html
How to Evaluate Journal Articles   http://lib.colostate.edu/howto/evaljrl.html
How to Evaluate a Web Page   http://lib.colostate.edu/howto/evalweb.html

Tips for Finding Materials on the Web

The Web is a useful resource for current topics. The recommended sources on the SPCC 200 pages have links to newspapers and useful Web sites. Make use of these.

If you wish to seek out information on the Web:
- Be aware of homographs—words spelled the same that mean something different. For example, "Mercury" can mean the car, god, element, or planet.
- Use advanced techniques when available. Look for advanced searching tips under "Help," "Advanced Searching," or "Searching Tips" on browser home pages.
- Use quotes around phrases. For example, "Rocky Mountain National Park"
- Use Boolean logic (AND, OR) when available. The browser or metasearch engine may refer to these as "all" (AND) or "any" (OR) of the words. For a detailed explanation of Boolean logic, see <http://lib.colostate.edu/howto/others/boolean.html>.

Current information is going to be found on news sites such as newspapers, television and radio stations. Links to a number of news sites are on <http://lib.colostate.edu/howto/late.html>. When you find information on one of these sites and if you think an article might be important, *print it out immediately!* News sites are updated constantly, and current news articles can disappear at any time—or may only be available for a fee. A Web address for a news site saved for a week— or even a day—frequently has an entirely different content by the time you get back to it.

Additional Strategies

- Once you find a useful article, use it to identify additional articles. See "Finding Articles on Similar Topics" for suggestions at <http://lib.colostate.edu/howto/simtop.html>.

- Figure out what type of journal your article is in by using the "Popular Magazines VS Trade Magazines VS Scholarly Journals" chart found on <http://lib.colostate.edu/howto/poplr.html>.

- Interviewing an expert or other knowledgeable person can be an excellent way to gather current information. Read "Interviews" for suggestions on how to identify someone to interview and to find out how to prepare for the interview at <http://lib.colostate.edu/howto/others/intervw.html>.

Point of View

Be sure to get as many different points of view as possible. Use articles from different journals and Web sites. Be careful; some organizations sponsor both journals and Web pages.

Creating the Works Cited Page
by Jennifer Emerling Bone and T.M. Linda Scholz

This information is based on MLA style, taken in part from *A Writer's Reference* by Diana Hacker.

- ✓ Begin on a NEW sheet of paper.
- ✓ Sources in the work cited page are ALWAYS alphabetized REGARDLESS of the type of source. DO NOT label or categorize the type of source used.
- ✓ List only sources that are cited in the speech.
- ✓ Double-space each entry.
- ✓ Indent additional lines of the same source five spaces.

Book
Author's last name first, title of the book (italicized or underlined), place of publication, publisher, and date.

Griffin, Cindy L. *Invitation to Public Speaking.* Belmont: Wadsworth, 2003.

Book by multiple authors
Name authors in the order in which they appear on the title page of the book. Reverse the name of ONLY the first author. Then, follow the above guidelines.

Morreale, Sherwin P., Brian H. Spitzberg, and J. Kevin Barge. *Human Communication:*

Motivation, Knowledge and Skills. Belmont: Wadsworth, 2001.

Unknown Author
Begin with the title, but do not use *A, An, The* as the starting word when you alphabetize entries.

The Pocket Oxford Spanish Dictionary. Oxford: Oxford UP, 1997.

Pamphlet
Cite as you would a book.

World Conference Against Racism: Racial Discrimination Xenophobia and Related

Intolerance. New York: United Nations Department of Public Information, 2001.

Magazine or Newspaper
Begin with authors name, title of the article in quotation marks, title of the source (magazine or newspaper) italicized or underlined, date (day, month and year), colon follows the year, page number/s.

Boyd, Valerie. "The Last Word." *Ms.* 25 Sept. 2000: 80-83.

Journal

Begin with authors name, title of the article in quotation marks, journal title (italicized or underlined), volume number, year of publication in parenthesis, colon follows the year, page numbers.

Keshishian, Flora. "Political Bias in Nonpolitical News: A Content Analysis of an

Armenian and Iranian Earthquake in the *New York Times* and *Washington Post*."

Critical Studies in Mass Communication 35 (1997): 332-43.

Personal Interview

Begin with the name of the person interviewed, then write "personal interview," and the date of the interview (day, month, year).

Loeffler-Clemens, Therese. Personal interview. 13 Dec. 2001.

E-mail

Author of the e-mail, topic of the e-mail in quotation marks, write "e-mail to _____," date

received.

Bone, Jennifer. "Creating a works cited page." E-mail to T. M. Linda Scholz. 14 Dec.

2001.

Television Educational Programs

Begin with the episode title in quotation marks, followed by the program title (underlined or italicized), the network, the local station and city, the broadcast date.

"Helping Women of the World." *Oprah.* ABC. KMGH, Denver. 3 Dec. 2001.

World Wide Web

Author, name of the article in quotation marks, title of the Webpage (underlined or italicized), the date of the last update/publication or date accessed, the electronic address in angle brackets.

Holland, Steve. "Bush: U. S. Abandoning Key 1972 Missile Treaty." *KUNC Community*

Radio for Northern Colorado. 13 Dec. 2001

<http://www.publicbroadcasting.net/kunc/news.newsmain>.

Encyclopedia

List the author of the article, title of the article, title of the encyclopedia/reference work (underlined or italicized), edition number and the date.

"Malcolm X." *The New American Desk Encyclopedia.* 1989.

Works Cited

Bone, Jennifer. "Creating a works cited page." E-mail to T. M. Linda Scholz. 14 Dec.

2001.

Boyd, Valerie. "The Last Word." *Ms.* 25 Sept. 2000: 80-83.

Griffin, Cindy L. *Invitation to Public Speaking.* Belmont: Wadsworth, 2003.

"Helping Women of the World." *Oprah.* ABC. KMGH, Denver. 3 Dec. 2001.

Holland, Steve. "Bush: U. S. Abandoning Key 1972 Missile Treaty." *KUNC Community

Radio for Northern Colorado.* 13 Dec. 2001

<http://www.publicbroadcasting.net/kunc/news.newsmain>.

Keshishian, Flora. "Political Bias in Nonpolitical News: A Content Analysis of an

Armenian and Iranian Earthquake in the *New York Times* and *Washington Post.*"

Critical Studies in Mass Communication 35 (1997): 332-43.

Loeffler-Clemens, Therese. Personal interview. 13 Dec. 2001.

"Malcolm X." *The New American Desk Encyclopedia.* 1989.

Morreale, Sherwin P., Brian H. Spitzberg, and J. Kevin Barge. *Human Communication:

Motivation, Knowledge and Skills.* Belmont: Wadsworth, 2001.

The Pocket Oxford Spanish Dictionary. Oxford: Oxford UP, 1997.

*World Conference Against Racism: Racial Discrimination Xenophobia and Related

Intolerance.* New York: United Nations Department of Public Information, 2001.

Audience Survey—Informative Speech

Name _____

Topic _____

1. What do you know about the topic?

2. Are you interested in this topic? Why/why not?

3. What would you like to hear about this topic?

PowerPoint Workshop
Creating professional visual support for your presentation

This information is designed for those familiar with the Windows environment but who have never used PowerPoint before. It walks you through the basic steps for conceptualizing, creating, and displaying your presentation.

<u>Conceptualizing the Presentation</u>

As you think about what you want to include in your PowerPoint presentation, remember to follow the guidelines for preparing and using visual aids:

➢ Keep them simple
➢ Use fonts that are easy to read
➢ Use color effectively
➢ Do not let the visual aid dominate your presentation—(that can happen easily with so many PowerPoint animation and sound effect options).
➢ Practice with them
➢ *Have a back-up plan if technology fails!!!*

<u>Creating the Presentation</u>

There are many ways to create a presentation in PowerPoint. This is one way to get started, but play around with the technology to find a system that works for you.

1. Launch the program. Under Format choose "Apply Design Template."
2. Choose a presentation design appropriate for your presentation. | OK |
3. Under Format choose a "Slide Layout" for your first slide.
   Tip: Begin and end with a blank slide unless you want to display words or images at the very beginning and end of your speech.

→ A note on *Views:* Look at the bottom left-hand corner of your screen. You'll see icons representing different ways to view your presentation. The three most useful are *slide view* (allows you to create and edit your slides), *slide sorter view* (allows you to see the presentation as a whole and edit slide order), and *slide show* (allows you to see the presentation as the audience sees it.) To switch back and forth between views, click on the appropriate icon.

→ Getting out of *Slide Show:* To end a show and return to slide view, right click and choose End Show.

4. To create the next slide, choose New Slide on the Common Tasks bar. You will be prompted to select and Autolayout. Let's examine some of the different layout options:
   (a) *Title Slide:* type in the title of your presentation and other introductory information
   (b) *List Slide:* highlight key points in a bulleted list, or deactivate the bullets for a phrase or quotation
   (c) *Table and Chart Slides:* create tables from scratch, or import them from another Microsoft program
   (d) *Image Slides:* insert clip art or pictures from the Web—alone or next to a bulleted list

→ Formats and fonts work the same here as they do on Microsoft Word—just use the toolbar to change fonts, spacing bullets, etc.

Right now, you know enough to create a basic presentation suitable for a professional speech. If you want to add a few "bells and whistles" to your speech, there are various animation options.

Animating the Presentation

1. Go to Slide Sorter view and choose your List Slide. Return to Slide View.
2. Highlight the list.
3. Go to Slide Show and choose Preset Animation. You'll see a range of animation options here. Play around with them and find one that is appropriate for your presentation.
   Tip: Some of the animation options have corresponding sound effects. Stay away from those that might be distracting during your speech.
4. It is useful to get a preview of what your animation will look and sound like. Go to Slide Show and choose Animation Preview. A small box will appear that previews your animation choices. You can move the box to a convenient viewing location by dragging it.

Inserting Images

1. Go to Slide Sorter view and choose your Image Slide. Return to Slide View.
2. Double click on the image.
3. You may Insert a new image from the Microsoft Clip Art file or Replace an existing image.
4. You may also insert an image you have saved on your computer (one retrieved from the Web or another source). Go to Insert, choose Picture, then choose From File. Find the folder containing your image and add it to your presentation.

Viewing and Displaying the Presentation

1. Make sure you are at the beginning of your presentation. Choose the first slide in Slide Sorter view, or scroll to the top of the presentation in Slide view.
2. Go to Slide Show.
3. Hit the space bar or the left mouse button to advance your presentation.
4. If you accidentally advance too far during your presentation, use the left arrow to go back to the previous slide.

Final Thoughts

➤ **Remember that technology can fail at any moment.** If you have visuals that are critical to your speech, it is a good idea to prepare simple transparencies that can serve as a back up in case of a technical malfunction.

➤ **Save your presentation on a new disk.** Disk corruption is common, so make sure your disk is in top condition before you come to class. This also protects against virus spread.

➤ **Be sure you know what version of PowerPoint is loaded onto the computer** you'll be using for your presentation. If you attempt to display a PowerPoint presentation in a version of the software that differs from where you prepared it, you risk compatibility errors (certain fonts and graphics may not display). It's a good idea to bring your presentation disk to class before you present and make sure it displays properly.

➤ **Practice your speech with your PowerPoint running.** Students often are surprised by how the software operates during the presentation, and some don't know how to solve common problems (like a slide advancing too far or a sound effect that's loud and intrusive). The library will allow you to use a laptop and LCD projector in a library reading room to practice your presentation with the technology.

➤ **Don't allow the computer to dominate your performance.** Talk directly to your audience, keep your eyes focused on them (not the computer), and step back to the screen when you need to gesture to a visual aid. Your audience's attention should be focused on you, not your visual aid.

After using a public computer it is a good idea to **scan your disk for viruses** before you open it up on your home computer. You don't want to corrupt your entire system!

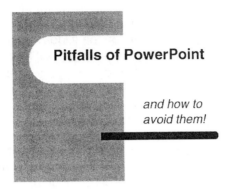

Pitfalls of PowerPoint

and how to avoid them!

Computer-generated visual support is a widely-used, and frequently abused technology. It can be a wonderful aid to public speakers but also has the potential to detract from your oral performance if used improperly. The following tips and suggestions will enable you to use computer-aided visual support in a productive way.

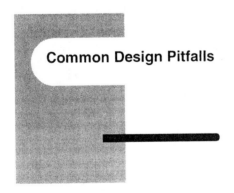

Common Design Pitfalls

✗ **Too much:** Too much of a good thing can turn into a bad thing. Just because your software allows you to introduce motion, sound effects, multiple backgrounds, and hidden slides doesn't mean you should give into the temptation. If your slides are too busy they might confuse or distract the audience. If they are noisy, they'll take the focus off you as a speaker. If they contain multiple hidden slides it will be easy for you to get off track during the presentation. <u>Remember the basic rule of VA design: Keep It Simple!</u>

✗ **Too wordy:** Your instructor likely uses PowerPoint to display outlines of class lectures with key terms and definitions. But class lectures have different goals than public speeches. In class, you need to be able to copy down exact terms and definitions. In a public speaking context, visual aids should enhance the clarity and interest value of your speech. They should be <u>visual *not* verbal</u> media. Do not simply display an outline of your speech for the class. Instead, use the computer to put up graphics, design charts and graphs, and even include short audio clips if appropriate for your topic.

✗ **Too advanced:** We try to keep our classroom equipment up to date, but this is (after all) a state university. We don't always have the most memory, the fastest processors, or the latest version of software. If your graphics are too large they may not load. If your presentation was prepared on a later version of the software, text and images may display differently (or not at all). If you're counting on a specific media player, it might not be loaded on the classroom computer. <u>Always check out a few sample slides *the class period before you speak* to ensure that our technology is compatible with your presentation.</u>

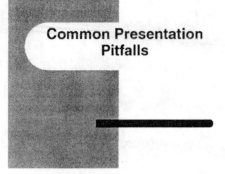

Common Presentation Pitfalls

✗ **Too dark:** It is common to turn out the lights when using PowerPoint, but that leads the audience to focus on the slides, not the speaker. <u>Choose a background that will display in a fully-lit room</u>.

✗ **Too technological:** Technology can be a useful and inexpensive way to display key information for your audience: a graphic you downloaded from a Website or a chart you designed to help your audience visualize the impact of your statistics. Just because you use PowerPoint, however, does not mean that you need a slide for every moment in your speech. Put up a few key images, insert blank slides in between so the images are not up longer than they need to be, and leave it at that. <u>You want the audience focus to stay on you, the speaker</u>.

✗ **Too distracted:** If you haven't practiced with your presentation, you often can get wrapped up in making it work during the speech. You focus intently on the keyboard, or turn your back on your audience and talk to the screen. Instead, <u>design a simple presentation that is easy to manage during your speech</u>. When you want to point to something specific on screen, step back, keep your shoulders facing the audience, and gesture broadly to the image. <u>Your integration of technology should be as seamless as your speech transitions</u>.

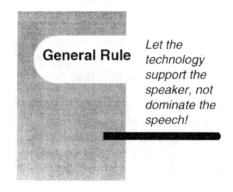

General Rule *Let the technology support the speaker, not dominate the speech!*

Sample Informative Speech Outline
for analysis and discussion

[Staple]

SPCC 200, [Section]
[Date]

Little Schoolhouse on the Prairie

by Kirsten Pullen and Josh Heuman˙

Specific Purpose Statement: To inform my audience about the one-room schoolhouse system.

Thesis: The one-room schoolhouse system is very different from the modern one: schools were primitive by today's standards, the curriculum was limited, and heavy demands were placed on the teacher.

Pattern of Organization: Topical

Introduction

I.   *[Attention-Getter]* Picture yourself in a small room with sixty other children ranging in age from six to thirteen.

   A.   The seats are hard, wooden benches.

   B.   The wind is howling outside, and the only heat comes from a wooden stove at the back of the room.

   C.   The teacher is frantically trying to keep the fire burning, entertain the younger children and discipline the older girls and boys, and cover the basics of reading, writing, and arithmetic.

II.   *[Reveal topic and relate to audience]* I've been describing a one-room schoolhouse—a classroom situation very different from the way most of us went to school.

   A.   Some of us may have thought our schools were out-of-date, and our teachers were overworked and frazzled.

   B.   But no matter how primitive our schools were, they were nothing like the schools on the prairie many of our grandparents and great-grandparents attended.

III.   *[Establish credibility]* I am interested in the one-room schoolhouse system for several reasons.

   A.   My grandmother taught school in one-room schoolhouses in Greenfield and Orient, Iowa during the 1920s.

   B.   In addition, I am an education major, and am committed to learning about past educational systems.

      1.   I have done research on this topic and I can tell you about this part of our pioneer heritage.

˙ **You will prepare all your speeches individually**, however, this outline was co-authored by two SPCC 200 instructors specifically for instructional use.

2. I attended mock school days led by my grandmother when I was in elementary school and junior high, so I have experienced the one-room schoolhouse system firsthand.

IV. [*Thesis & Preview*] Today I will tell you about three important facets of the one-room schoolhouse system: building the schools, establishing the curriculum, and the demands placed on a typical teacher.

Signpost: First, we'll look at how these schoolhouses were built.

Body

I. One-room schoolhouses were originally inexpensive, transitional buildings, usually made of logs or planks; eventually one-room school houses became permanent structures made of brick.

[*visual aid*: cross-section pictures of log and plank schools]

A. At the beginning of the nineteenth-century, one-room schoolhouses were constructed from log.

1. The log cabin school did not require any money to build, and the process of building a log cabin school was really quite simple, according to school historian E. Wayne Fuller.

a. A family donated land for the school, and people from the town volunteered their help.

b. Most one-room schoolhouses were under twenty-five feet long.

c. The roof was made from clapboards attached to poles that ran the length of the building.

d. Logs were notched at the ends and cemented together to form the building walls.

i. In her history of American fires, Nadine Taran notes that these school and their students were particularly susceptible to accidental immolation.

e. The door was made from rough boards and hung on leather or wood hinges.

2. Again according to E. Wayne Fuller, most log cabin schools were extremely primitive.

a. The floors were dirt, the windows were covered with oiled paper, and the room was mostly filled with the fireplace.

b. Schoolhouses contained no flags, bells, maps, chalkboards, or even desks—nothing that signifies "school" to us today.

i. Writing tables were supported by pegs in the cabin walls, so most children had to stand while writing.

ii. The schools could not afford maps, chalkboards, flags, or bells.

B. By the middle of the nineteenth-century, pioneer society had grown more complex as more settlers moved west, and these log cabin schools were no longer sufficient.

1. E. Wayne Fuller explains that log cabins were replaced by plank schools.

a. Much more thought went into constructing these schools.

       i.   Everyone in town met and decided upon a spot to build the school.

       ii. They planned exactly how the school would be built.

    b. These schools were made of planks at least two inches thick.

  2. Internally, these schools changed dramatically.

    a. They contained cast-iron stoves, glass windows, and wooden floors.

    b. The desks and chairs were store-bought rather than made by hand.

    c. Some schools even spent money for chalkboards and maps.

C. Fuller *also* explains how towards the end of the nineteenth century, some towns built brick school houses.

  1. One-room schoolhouses never got any better than this.

    a. Only the richest areas could build these schools.

       i.   These schools were much more expensive to build, and supported by taxes.

       ii. Therefore, plank schools remained the most common.

    b. Brick schoolhouses contained maps and chalkboards, hooks to hang coats and hats, more comfortable desks, and private bathrooms.

  2. By the end of the Depression, one-room schoolhouses—whether made of logs, planks, or bricks, had mostly disappeared from the American landscape.

Transition: More important than the exterior of the schools was what was taught inside.

II. Within the one-room schoolhouse system, the Four "Rs"—reading, writing, arithmetic and recitation—were the core components of the curriculum.

A. Historian of education <u>Andrew Guildford</u> tells how reading, which also included grammar and spelling, was the most important part of the curriculum.

  1. The standard teaching tool was a small book called a primer, which combined reading, grammar, and spelling.

  2. After students had mastered primers, they moved onto readers.

  3. Grammar was taught by exercises in phrasing and diagramming.

    a. Diagramming taught students proper use of adverbs, adjectives, and prepositional phrases.

    b. Teachers expected students to memorize grammar rules, but students were hardly ever tested on them.

    c. This is unlike most of our schools, where we're tested on grammar from elementary school through high school graduation!

  4. Spelling recitations were daily rituals in most schools.

    a. Many of the words were long and unpronounceable.

    b. Guildford claims that "the ability to spell words correctly was highly prized by the community, but little concern was given to whether or not the students actually knew what the words meant."

B. Writing developed as another key aspect of schools.

1. Only cursive writing was taught—no printing allowed!

2. At the beginning of the nineteenth century, students learned a beautiful cursive, but by the end of the century a more vertical writing was used, according to historian <u>H. Robert Bremer</u>.

3. Teachers stressed that writing neatly was an essential skill.

C. Arithmetic was the most practical subject taught in the schools—children needed to understand math for use on their farms.

D. The fourth curricular component was recitation—remembering and repeating information taught to in the schools.

   1. Recitation played a prominent role in the school curriculum.

      a. The dearth of textbooks and paper made memorization important.

      b. And, according to schoolteacher <u>Lucille Meisenheimer</u> in a 1954 article in *Life* magazine, educators believed the mind was like a muscle—if it was not continually used, it might lose its knowledge.

   2. Many schools held annual recitation contests, with prizes given to students who were able to recite the longest and most difficult passages.

Internal Summary and Transition: We've heard about the different kinds of one-room schoolhouses, and the kinds of subjects studied inside. Now, let's consider the one person who brought it all together: the teacher.

III. Selecting a new teacher required the community to work together to determine who best fit their needs, according to the website <u>"Teaching in a One-Room School."</u>

A. Teachers had to do more than just lead in the classroom.

   1. Teachers were role models for both the young and old.

   2. They were expected to organize social events, plan debates, create special programs, and be upstanding citizens with high moral values.

B. Teachers were often strong-minded, independent women who did not depend on others.

   1. Most teachers were women.

      a. Though the pay was low, teaching was one of the few jobs open to women, according to my grandmother.

      b. Teaching gave women status, respectability, and a feeling of accomplishment.

   2. Most teachers quit work after they married.

      a. Many women started teaching as young as sixteen, often getting married in four or five years and starting families of their own.

      b. According to <u>my grandmother</u>, she kept her engagement to my grandfather secret for nine months.

         i. She was afraid that if the school board knew she was getting married, they'd give the job to a single girl.

         ii. In fact, after my grandmother married, she was "released" from her teaching contract.

iii. However, she was lucky to find work in another town, and continued to add her income to the family farm.

C. The schools provided living accommodations and few benefits along with a small salary to the teachers.

   1. A teacher's pay included room and board, but a teacher would travel from home to home, sharing a bed with one or more children, remembered Lucille Meisenheimer.

   2. The school board also promised to teacher to keep the schoolhouses in good repair and furnish the fuel—though the teachers had to tend the fires themselves.

   3. Teachers had no sick leave or pensions.

   4. There were no unions—and definitely no strikes!

D. One-room schoolhouse teachers were able to work without being required to complete the kinds of college courses teachers today must.

   1. In the early part of the nineteenth-century, a girl could begin to teach as soon as she passed the eighth-grade comprehensive tests.

   2. As time went on, state laws required teacher certification.

      a. My grandmother told me that even as late as the 1920s, all a girl had to do was take three days of exams, proctored by the school board and the county superintendent.

      b. A passing score qualified a person to teach without a single day of supervised teaching experience!

      c. According to Andrew Guildford, this system insured that the teachers knew the subject matter, but didn't necessarily mean they knew how to teach it.

   3. Though some young women graduated from college or attended some teaching classes, most were able to further their education and experience only at Teachers Institutes offered by state school superintendents during the summer months.

Conclusion

I. [*Signal End*] As we've seen today,

II. [*Review*] one-room schoolhouses are very different from the schools we attended.

A. Our teachers do not have to teach eight different grades at once, while keeping a fire burning and traveling from home to home.

B. Our schools are warm, modern buildings, and we have access to textbooks, paper, chalkboards—even computers.

C. Our curriculum is more than the reading, writing, and arithmetic, and recititation is no longer a priority.

D. Our communities no longer expect our teachers to be civic leaders, and they no longer have to be unmarried women.

III. [*Closing line*] I encourage you to see if there is an old school house near your home open to tours, or talk to your grandparents about their experiences—my old high school doesn't seem so bad when I compare it to the schools of just sixty years ago!

[page break between speech and works cited page]

Works Cited

Bremer, H. Robert. *Children and Youth in America: A Documentary History*. Oxford and New York: Basil Blackwell Ltd., 1998.

Fuller, E. Wayne. *One-Room Schools of the Middle West*. New York: Harper and Row. 1989.

Guildford, Andrew. *America's Country Schools*. Los Angeles: Berkeley UP, 1997.

McBride, Ruth. Personal Interview. 13 Sep 2000.

Meisenheimer, Lucille. "Memoirs of a Country School Teacher." *Life* 3:14 (July 1954). 61-66.

Taran, Nadine. "Fires in America: 1620–1918." *The American History Project*.

<http://www.ahp.org/taran.htm> (21 Sep 2000).

Checklist for Complete Sentence Outlines

 I'm stapled.

• I have a heading with speech title, name, department and course number, section number, and date

• I have an explicit and well thought out thesis statement and method of organization appropriate to the content of the speech.

• I have a complete introduction and conclusion, with each part labeled.

• I'm held together with strong internal structure and my connectives are labeled.

• My 2–5 main points are parallel and distinct, divide the topic logically, and are presented in main point topic sentences. …

• … as are my 2–5 subpoints within each main point.

• My subordinate points are subordinate to their superordinates.

• I include sufficient research to offer an interesting and comprehensive picture of my topic (supporting material in each main point).

• My works cited page conforms to the MLA guidelines outlined in this coursebook.

• There are two copies to submit to the instructor, with a works cited page attached to each.

Topic Proposal: Informative Speech

Name: _____

Propose two potential topics for your Informative Speech. List them below, in order of preference, and explain what strategies you would use to adapt each topic to your class audience.

Topic 1:
Specific purpose:

Thesis statement:

Proposed speech main points:

What specific strategies will you use to make this speech compelling for your audience?

Topic 2:
Specific purpose:

Thesis statement:

Proposed speech main points:

What specific strategies will you use to make this speech compelling for your audience?

Instructor Comments: Topic 1 _____Approved _____Not Approved
                              Topic 2 _____Approved _____Not Approved

Critique Sheet: Informative Speech

Speaker _____

Topic _____

+	Excellent
✓	Satisfactory
--	Needs improvement
0	Failed to complete

Specific strengths and areas for improvement:

INTRODUCTION
Gained audience's attention _____
Established credibility _____
Introduced topic clearly _____
Related topic to audience _____
Concise thesis/preview _____

BODY
Main points clear _____
Main points fully supported _____
Sufficient source citations _____
Language clear & concise _____
Transitions clear _____

CONCLUSION
Signaled ending of speech _____
Summarized main points _____
Ended with artistic last line _____

DELIVERY
Maintained eye contact _____
Used vocal variety _____
Projected adequately _____
Pronunciation correct _____
Articulation clear _____
Rate appropriate _____
Paused effectively _____
Gestures purposeful _____
Mannerisms appropriate _____
Facial expression _____
Extemporaneous style _____
Effective speaking notes _____

VISUAL AIDS
Clear & easy to see _____
Professionally designed _____
Aesthetically appealing _____
Visual, rather than verbal _____
Incorporated well into the
 speech _____
Technology used
 appropriately _____

OUTLINE

Complete sentence format	_____
Logical subordination	_____
Labels included	_____
Works cited page	_____
Spelling accurate	_____
Grammatically correct	_____
Free of typographical errors	_____

OVERALL EVALUATION

Topic challenging	_____
Speech adapted to audience	_____
Completed in time limit	_____

Instructor comments and suggestions:

TIME _____

Score _____ **/200**

Listening Sheet: Inform Speech
Research

Listener:

Speaker: Topic:

During the speech, record the speaker's source citations , of supporting material.
Then, reflect on the quality of the research as it related to aker's credibility and audience
adaptation.

Front page: complete during the speech
Sources:

Citation   Type of Research

Back page: complete after the speech is done
Did the speaker cite sources clearly throughout the speech?

Which main points were particularly well supported with research?

Which main points would have benefited from more support?

Which source citation(s) contributed most to the speaker's credibility? Why?

Which source citation(s) helped the speaker adapt to her/his class audience? Why?

What could the speaker have done differently with his/her sources to improve speaker credibility and audience adaptation?

**Listening Sheet: Informative Speech
Delivery**

Listener:

Speaker: Topic:

Identify 2 of the speaker's delivery *strengths* (comment on volume, pitch, rate, pauses, vocal variety, pronunciation, articulation, dialect, appearance, bodily action, gestures, and eye contact).

Identify 2 *areas for improvement* in the speaker's delivery (comment on volume, pitch, rate, pauses, vocal variety, pronunciation, articulation, dialect, appearance, bodily action, gestures, and eye contact).

What speech preparation or practice techniques would you recommend to the speaker to improve her/his delivery?

**Listening Sheet: Informative Speech
Visual Aid Design**

Listener:

Speaker: Topic:

Evaluate the quality of the speaker's visual aid <u>design</u>.
     Were VAs aesthetically appealing? Why or why not?

In what ways did VA design enhance or detract from the clarity of the message?

Were the VAs in this speech suitable for a professional context? If not, what would you suggest the speaker do differently?

**Listening Sheet: Informative Speech
Visual Aid Use**

Listener:

Speaker: Topic:

Comment on how well the speaker <u>used</u> visual aids within his/her speech?
    Did the speaker work with VAs smoothly and confidently?

Evaluate the speaker's eye contact and bodily action as s/he worked with VAs.

How well did the speaker work with VA props and/or technology? (VA stand, overhead
projector, computer, etc.)

Self-Evaluation Sheet: Informative Speech

Name:_____Topic:_____

1. What do you feel were the major strengths of the CONTENT of your speech?
   (comment on organization, connectives, source citation, and visual aid)

2. What do you feel were the major weaknesses of the CONTENT of your speech?

3. What do you feel were the best aspects of your speech's DELIVERY?
   (comment on volume, pitch, rate, pauses, vocal variety, pronunciation, articulation, dialect, kinesics, appearance, bodily action, gestures, and eye contact)

4. What aspects of your speech's DELIVERY would you like to improve?

5. What elements of this speech do you feel were improved from your last speech?

6. Give an example of how/where/when you might use this type of speech in your future.

7. Has your level of nervousness changed since your last speech? Why or why not?

UNIT FOUR: INVITATIONAL SPEAKING

> 📄 **Reading:** *Invitation to Public Speaking,* Ch. 16

Unit Objectives: After completing this unit you should understand:

✓ how to enter into a dialogue with your audience in order to explore a complex issue

✓ how to appreciate multiple perspectives

✓ how to create a communication environment that allows your audience to participate in a meaningful and productive way

Assignment: Invitational Dialogue

You will prepare a short (4-5 minute) speech to explore an issue or articulate a position. That speech will be delivered before a small group of class colleagues, who will then participate with you in a mini invitational dialogue (10 minutes total for the speech and dialogue). Your topic should be potentially suitable for the policy speech assignment, and you should use the invitational dialogue as an opportunity to 1) find a topic for your policy speech, and 2) gain a greater understanding of and appreciation for your audience's diverse perspectives before you design your policy speech. The invitational dialogue assignment has *3 graded components:*

1. On the day of the class dialogues, turn in two copies of a <u>typed outline</u> of your invitational speech with <u>dialogue question prompts</u> listed at the end.
2. During the workshop, complete the invitational dialogue <u>feedback sheets</u> included in this coursebook.
3. After class, write a <u>paper assessing the exercise</u> that conforms to your instructor's specifications.

Because the invitational approach assumes that each member of the class community has something valuable to contribute to the dialogue, <u>your presence and participation in this class workshop is required</u> in order to earn points for this assignment.

The Invitational Dialogue Emphasizes the Following Skills:

⇨ Organization: a dialogue can be organized to facilitate clear and comprehensive exploration of an issue

⇨ Dialogue: before you can ethically and effectively persuade an audience, you must appreciate the multiple sides to every issue and value your audience members' unique perspectives

⇨ Speaker Credibility: in order for audience members to value your opinion, they must feel that you respect them. You can demonstrate this by creating conditions of equality, value, and self-determination

⇨ Audience Adaptation: when audience members feel that you respect them as equals, you value their views, and you will allow them to determine their own courses of action, they are more likely to participate in communicative exchanges in an authentic and meaningful way

Why It's Important: Appreciating Multiple Perspectives

The skills you will learn in the invitational speaking unit will serve you well in a variety of professional and personal contexts. Consider the following scenarios:

↝ You and your parents never discuss politics because you're both so far apart on the issues you just end up having the same fight over and over. One day, you begin a conversation by asking your dad to tell you about the time he was passed over for a promotion and a female colleague got it instead. After he finishes his story, you tell him about an experience a friend of yours had when she was sexually harassed on the job. You both leave the conversation with a broader understanding of a complex social issue. Although neither one of you has changed your mind, the mutual respect you gained by listening to one another will allow you to continue the dialogue in the future.

↝ You and your partner are having a familiar argument about who should be in charge of various chores at home. Instead of trying to convince your partner that you are right, you ask him/her to explain what's going on in his/her life that makes it difficult to find the time to pitch in around the house. Feeling validated by your genuine concern, your partner asks you the same question. The conversation allows both of you to frame the problem differently. Rather than asking the question, "how can we split housework equally?" you both ask the question, "how can we work together to achieve our goals both inside and outside the home? How can we maximize each other's skills and minimize each other's frustrations?"

↝ You have been promoted to a management position at work. Your predecessor was let go because of his inability to get the staff to work together and maintain high productivity. In your first staff meeting, you conduct a dialogue with your staff using the principles of equality, value, and self-determination. The staff provides you with valuable insight about their specific jobs, knowledge that you never could obtain without performing each job personally. In addition, because you began your meeting by asking for their input, your staff feels more invested in the organization. Open lines of communication foster respect and loyalty, which in turn helps the staff function more effectively.

↝ You are a member of your local school board. The board is being asked to consider a new science curriculum. Aspects of the curriculum, such as the origins of the universe and the nature of human life, are controversial. You do not have special training in science or philosophy but you want to make a decision that serves the community in a fair and responsible way. Before the board votes, you convene a hearing in which members of the community with special insight into science, philosophy, religion, and education are invited to share their perspective on the appropriateness of the proposed curriculum. Not only do you broaden your knowledge base before voting on the new curriculum, you also give opponents and supporters of the measure an equal opportunity to be heard. If the vote does not go their way, they at least will know that members of the their community value their perspective and include them in discussions.

**Invitational Dialogue
Feedback**

Speaker's Name: _____

Topic: _____

Speech type:
_____ explore an issue
_____ articulate a position

In what ways, if at all, did this speaker create an invitational speaking environment (conditions of equality, value, and self-determination).

List examples of invitational language you heard in this person's speech. If there were none, identify language choices that may have inhibited the invitational environment.

Can you suggest strategies the speaker could have used to enhance the invitational environment during their speech and dialogue?

What question(s) or concern(s) did you have about the speaker's topic after hearing the speech?

Invitational Dialogue
Feedback

Speaker's Name: _____

Topic: _____

Speech type:
_____ explore an issue
_____ articulate a position

In what ways, if at all, did this speaker create an invitational speaking environment (conditions of equality, value, and self-determination).

List examples of invitational language you heard in this person's speech. If there were none, identify language choices that may have inhibited the invitational environment.

Can you suggest strategies the speaker could have used to enhance the invitational environment during their speech and dialogue?

What question(s) or concern(s) did you have about the speaker's topic after hearing the speech?

Invitational Dialogue
Feedback

Speaker's Name: _____ _____

Topic: _____

Speech type:
_____ explore an issue
_____ articulate a position

In what ways, if at all, did this speaker create an invitational speaking environment (conditions of equality, value, and self-determination).

List examples of invitational language you heard in this person's speech. If there were none, identify language choices that may have inhibited the invitational environment.

Can you suggest strategies the speaker could have used to enhance the invitational environment during their speech and dialogue?

What question(s) or concern(s) did you have about the speaker's topic after hearing the speech?

**Invitational Dialogue
Feedback**

Speaker's Name: _____

Topic: _____

Speech type:
_____ explore an issue
_____ articulate a position

In what ways, if at all, did this speaker create an invitational speaking environment (conditions of equality, value, and self-determination).

List examples of invitational language you heard in this person's speech. If there were none, identify language choices that may have inhibited the invitational environment.

Can you suggest strategies the speaker could have used to enhance the invitational environment during their speech and dialogue?

What question(s) or concern(s) did you have about the speaker's topic after hearing the speech?

UNIT FIVE: PERSUASIVE SPEAKING

> 🗎 **Reading:** *Invitation to Public Speaking,* Ch. 8, 17-18

Unit Objectives: After completing this unit you should understand:

- ✓ how persuasive speaking is different from informative or invitational speaking

- ✓ how to adapt to an audience that might be unconcerned about or opposed to your ideas

- ✓ how to build an argument with evidence

- ✓ effective methods of reasoning

- ✓ how to appeal to emotions

- ✓ the types of organization for persuasive speeches

Assignment: Policy Speech

Prepare and present a 6-8 minute speech that proposes a plan to solve a current public problem. After your 8 minute speech, field 2-3 minutes worth of questions from the audience. You may arrange your policy speech into either then problem-solution organizational pattern or the problem-cause-solution pattern. Make sure to relate your discussion of the problem and proposed solution specifically to your class audience. Cite at least 6-8 different <u>sources</u> for your audience during the speech (underline or highlight them on your outline). Prior to the delivery of the speech, submit 2 copies of a typed complete-sentence outline, including a works cited page. Avoid spelling, typographical, or grammatical errors.

The Policy Speech Assignment Emphasizes the Following Skills:

- ⇨ Organization: Choose an organizational pattern that suits your topic and persuasive goals.

- ⇨ Argument: Well-developed arguments should support your persuasive claims. Include clear logical appeals, appropriate emotional appeals, and thorough research.

- ⇨ Speaker Credibility: Every aspect of your performance, from topic selection to research to delivery, should evidence your personal credibility as a speaker.

- ⇨ Audience Adaptation: Your speech should show evidence of careful audience analysis and specific audience adaptation. Anticipate and respond to potential counterarguments against your proposed plan.

- ⇨ Visual Support: Visual aids are optional this time, but strongly suggested. Visual support can help illustrate and support your persuasive claims.

Why It's Important: Learning to Advocate for Change

Part of being a responsible citizen is being prepared to advocate for change when change is needed. Many people would prefer to be "armchair quarterbacks" when it comes to solving problems in their home, school, workplace, or community. It is easy to debunk other people's proposals for change. It's tougher to come up with a constructive, workable solution to a problem. The policy speech assignment is designed to teach skills vital to democratic citizenship: identifying a problem that affects other people, coming up with a workable and beneficial plan for change, and convincing others that they should support your course of action.

Skills learned from the policy speech are not just relevant for the "politically minded." There are many times in our lives when the ability to argue for a specific policy could benefit us personally. Negotiating for flex time at work, participating in a homeowner's association or athletic league board, advocating that your local gym change its class schedule—each of these scenarios involves the advocacy skills on which we focus in this unit. When you become a credible advocate for change, you empower yourself, benefit others, and experience the positive changes that occur as a result of your efforts.

☑ **Tips & Suggestions: The Argument Triangle**

CLAIM

EVIDENCE   **ANALYSIS**

The argument triangle provides a simple but concrete way to visualize how you should develop arguments in your policy speech. Every argument has three components: 1) a clear persuasive claim, 2) evidence from your research that supports and illustrates the claim, and 3) your own analysis that connects the evidence to the claim. Evaluate each main point in your speech. Every one should begin with a clear claim that is supported with evidence that *directly* proves your claim. Round out each main point with your own analysis.

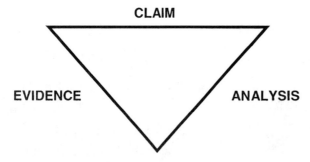

CLAIM: "Nitrate levels have been increasing in our water for years, and this situation is clearly dangerous."

EVIDENCE: "As indicated by the *Colorado Farm Journal*, pollution levels have gone from 2.3% in 1970 to 12.8% in 1998."

The *Greeley Tribune* reported: "Holes, as well as seepage from waste lagoons, overcrowding of animals, and lack of quality sewage systems are adding to the ever-increasing problem."

ANALYSIS: As Colorado's front range continues to become more populated, this problem will affect more and more of us.

Advocating for a Policy:
Need, Plan, and Practicality by AnnaMarie Adams Mann

The first step in understanding questions of policy is to know which *issues* you, as a speaker, must address when advocating for a specific policy change. There are three issues that must be addressed: **NEED, PLAN, and PRACTICALITY.**

<u>NEED</u>: Before presenting a policy or plan of action, you must demonstrate that a current problem exists and that it relates to your specific audience. To support this claim, you must use credible evidence (i.e. examples, statistics, narratives, definitions, and/or testimonies) that illustrates the severity of the problem and, simultaneously, connects the problem to the audience. Information relevant to the need argument includes (but may not be limited to) the following:

- A general explanation of the problem
- The population that is effected by the problem
- The severity of the problem
- The dangers involved if the problem is not fixed

<u>PLAN</u>: Now that you have persuaded your audience that there is a "need" for change, the next step is to present a plan that responds to this "need." An effective plan not only solves the problem, but also addresses questions such as: Who will implement the plan? Who will enforce the plan? Who will fund the plan? Although the presentation of a plan will vary by context, the format below may provide a good starting point:

- <u>Explain your plan</u>: What does your plan entail? What are the specific courses of action you advocate implementing?
- <u>State whom will enforce the plan</u>: For example, if regulating the nutritional value of fast food, would you rely on the industry to police itself or would you require the FDA (Food and Drug Administration) to enforce it?
- <u>Discuss funding</u>: Remember, funding doesn't have to always come from taxes. Sometimes the money needed to support a policy comes from reallocating existing funds.

<u>PRACTICALITY</u>: When presenting a plan, a speaker must also demonstrate that the plan is practical and, thus, the best solution to employ. To show the practicality of a plan, you will need to address three areas:

- <u>Cure</u>: does the "plan" solve the problems presented in the "need" section of your speech? You can support this claim by providing examples of your plan successfully implemented in other contexts, citing expert testimony that suggests your plan is a recommended course of action, drawing analogies that illustrate why your plan is a good response to the problem, and/or and providing statistics or other evidence that supports your reasoning.
- <u>Advantages outweigh disadvantages</u>: with every plan, disadvantages are going to arise. As the speaker, it is your responsibility to show how the advantages/benefits of the plan outweigh the disadvantages/costs. Remember, costs can be monetary but can also be measured in other ways (such as loss of liberty, ethical costs, etc.).
- <u>Counterarguments</u>: when persuading an audience, counterarguments are bound to arise. In order to stop those counterarguments from snowballing and interfering with your persuasive appeal, you can address them in your speech and follow with a statement that contests that argument.

Fitting Need, Plan, and Practicality into an Organizational Pattern

Now that you understand the three issues that need to be addressed when advocating for a policy, you need to know how this information relates to the organizational patterns used to write a policy speech. Two examples are provided below:

Problem-Solution

If using a problem-solution pattern, your body will consist of two main points. The first main point should address the problem that you are presenting to your audience. As such, you will develop your "need" arguments in this main point. The second main point should address the solution and, therefore, should include both the "plan" and the "practicality" of your plan.

BODY

I.   **Problem (includes need)**
II.   **Solution (includes plan and practicality)**

Problem-Cause-Solution

If using a problem-solution pattern, your body will consist of three main points. The first main point should address the problem that you are presenting to your audience. As such, you will include your evidence supporting the "need" in this main point. The second main point should detail the cause of the problem. Similar to the first main point, the cause will be supported with evidence you gathered to support the "need" for a plan. The third main point addresses the solution and, therefore, should include both the "plan" and the "practicality" of your plan.

BODY

I.   **Problem (includes need)**
II.   **Cause (includes need)**
III.   **Solution (includes plan and practicality)**

Fielding Questions After a Persuasive Speech

There are many situations that require the ability to field questions in a calm and convincing manner—job interviews, training sessions, professional presentations, and interpersonal debates. The purpose of Q&A in this class is to familiarize you with strategies for fielding questions successfully, and to expose you to an actual Q&A session.

Objectives of the Q&A session:
- Clarify information
- Expand or reinforce your arguments
- Bolster your credibility
- Assuage listener concerns

Q&A Frame of Mind:

Competence

A question session should showcase your communication competence. Reinforce your claims for the audience and be prepared to explain and extend your arguments with new examples and additional evidence. There is usually information that you cannot include in your speech due to time constraints—this is your opportunity to share that information with the audience.

Never fake it—audiences can spot a phony a mile away. Be willing to admit areas of ignorance by saying something like, "That's an aspect of the topic I haven't considered in depth," or "That's a good suggestion. I would like to pursue that in further research."

Collaboration

A question session is <u>not</u> a confrontation. You want to win over your audience, not beat them in an argument. Even though some audience members might bait you and try to engage you in confrontation, do not risk it. You will end up undermining your own credibility if you go "one-on-one" with a listener. Instead, emphasize areas of convergence between your arguments and the questioner's position. Listen carefully to the questions that are posed. Be willing to admit areas of ignorance or weaknesses in your argument. Remember, the effectiveness of a speech is judged by how well it is adjusted to the audience.

Control

When you are the speaker, you get to control the presentation. If you need a moment or two to think about a question before you respond, take it! Do not relinquish control of your topic by "buying into" someone else's premise. Do not allow one questioner to dominate the Q&A session—acknowledge others after you have given one audience member the opportunity for a question and follow-up question/response.

Common Sense

Do not feel that everyone is "out to get you" after you have given a speech. People have different motivations for asking questions—to seek clarification, to make themselves look smart, to help you support your claims, or to contradict you. Not all questions are hostile. That is why listening is an especially important skill during a Q&A session.

Q&A Strategies:

- Answer Format:
  1. Listen for the concept and assess the questioner's motivation.
  2. Restate the question aloud if it needs clarification or if you want to make sure you are interpreting it correctly.
  3. State your answer succinctly.
  4. Support your answer→ reiterate what you said in your speech or offer new information or evidence.

- Nonverbal Behavior:
  ➢ As you answer a question, look at the questioner first, but also scan the whole audience.
  ➢ Maintain a firm, authoritative stance. Try to minimize distracting gestures and movements.
  ➢ Try to look and feel relaxed.

- Responding to specific types of questions:
  ➢ *Loaded questions:* "Don't you know that environmental regulation costs jobs?" Acknowledge the listener's position/emotions. State your position without buying into the listener's premise. Try to emphasize areas of convergence between the two positions.

    Ex: "It sounds like you're concerned about the economic implications of my proposal. That's understandable since previous regulations have had a negative effect on local economies. In fact, that was on of my main concerns as I was researching and developing this plan. However, by training businesses to use the environment more efficiently, I'm ensuring that the resources they need to keep their businesses going will be in plentiful supply for years to come. Without some sort of change in how businesses interact with the environment, local companies will have to shut down or move operations out of this region in just ten to twenty years."

  ➢ *Complex questions:* "I wonder which regulatory measures are best, most effective, and how much each costs?" State that the question has several parts, and you will answer it piece by piece. Do not feel compelled to answer every issue. Feel free to focus on the most important/relevant question(s).

  ➢ *Vague questions:* "What do you think about NAFTA?" Clarify with the questioner what s/he is trying to find out about before you attempt to answer.

  ➢ *Statement of open disagreement/hostility:* "I can't believe you cited something from PETA—they are the most radical animal rights group around. They care more about animals than people!" Tell the listener you understand how s/he feels, answer the specific objection, find areas of convergence if possible, then move on to another question. Never allow hostility to escalate.

Sample Policy Speech Outline
for analysis and discussion

[Staple]

SPCC 200, [Section]
[Date]

Solving Our Nitrate Problem
By Julie Kreps

Specific Purpose Statement: To persuade my audience that nitrate poisoning in our water is a serious problem that could be solved by encouraging the development of smaller hog farms.

Thesis: Nitrite poisoning is a serious threat to public health, one that is exacerbated by large, corporate hog farms. We can substantially reduce this problem by adopting a plan to encourage smaller, more numerous hog farms, as opposed to massive corporate operations.

Pattern of Organization: Problem/Cause/Solution

Introduction

I.   [*Attention-Getter*] Imagine that you are on a trip to your favorite fishing hole for a relaxing day in the sun. You stroll down to the bank, fishing pole in hand, whistling your favorite tune.

    A.   You reach the shore, excited for your long-awaited vacation, and then it hits you.

    B.   All along the banks are dead and rotting fish, lining the shore for hundreds of feet.

    C.   Your mouth drops as the park ranger explains how manure from the local hog farm has polluted the water with nitrates and killed the entire fish population.

II. [*Reveal topic and relate to audience*] Unfortunately, our imaginary trip to a polluted fishing hole is far from fanciful. Rising nitrate levels in our lakes, streams, and drinking water is a very real problem here in Colorado.

III. [*Establish* credibility] I have done extensive research on hog-farm issues and have attended numerous conferences on the issue of animal-waste runoff.

IV. [*Thesis &* Preview] Something must be done to reduce the threat of toxic nitrate levels in our water. Today, I will argue that:

    A. Nitrate poisoning is a serious threat to public health—one that can potentially affect each and every one of us.

    B. The problem of nitrate poisoning is exacerbated by large, corporate hog farms.

    C. We can substantially reduce this problem by adopting a plan to encourage smaller, more numerous hog farms, as opposed to massive corporate operations.

Body

I. (Problem/Need)[Signpost] First, nitrate levels have been increasing in our water for years, and this situation is clearly dangerous.

    A.   A nitrate is a gaseous compound created by the fermentation of animal bi-products.

    B.   As indicated by the *Colorado Farm Journal*, pollution levels have gone from 2.3% in 1970 to 12.8% in 1998.

        1.   The *Greeley Tribune* reported: "Holes, as well as seepage from waste lagoons, overcrowding of animals, and lack of quality sewage systems are adding to the ever-increasing problem."

        2.   One large source of water that is currently being affected is the underground aquifers in the eastern part of Colorado.

        3.   As a *US News & World Report* article disclosed, "If nitrate levels continue to rise at this same rate over the next decade, more than 38% of the current water supplies will be unsuitable for human use."

Transition: Obviously, nitrate levels are rising dramatically, but why should we care?

    C.   High nitrate levels are very poisonous, especially to infants and sensitive aquatic life.

        1.   According to the *Soil Science Society of America*, "blue baby disease, from infected red blood cells, is a direct result of toxic nitrate levels."

    D.   High nitrate levels are also deadly to fish.

        1.   Christopher Thorne stated that "Manure runoff has been the culprit of massive fish kills of over 60,000 fish along Colorado waterways."

II. (Cause/Need) [*Transition*] At the head of this problem are the factory-sized hog farms.

    A.   Some of the larger operations can hold up to 10,000 head of hogs on a single site.

    B.   As you can see on this chart from *National Hog Farms*, waste production is overflowing the space available for its disposal. [The speaker then displayed a bar graph to support her argument.]

        1.   This is roughly the amount of waste created from the number of people in Larimer County, confined to an area the size of CSU campus.

    D.   According to the Megahogs web site, "none of the regulations applicable to the smallest city waste disposal system apply to hog factory lagoons."

E. A recent article entitled "Monitoring Hog Farms" stated that "six miscarriages were traced to the water from the manure produced at a local hog farm."

   1. Once these women stopped drinking the water from their wells, they delivered healthy babies.

III. (Solution/Plan) [*Internal preview*] I propose a plan, involving both state and national governments, to help regenerate the number of smaller hog-producing farms and curtail large-scale hog factories.

A. First of all, local governments, along with some nationally funded programs, would allow tax breaks to small producers who are just beginning to raise hogs.

   1. This plan would target two groups:

      a. It would target young men and women who are just beginning to assemble their operations.

      b. And it would also target those who combine hog raising with growing corn, wheat, soybeans, and other hog feeds.

         i. This tax break would include a lower rate of taxation on agricultural commodities; however, this break would only target small families whose income depends on farm commodities.

B. In the next step of the plan, each state government would establish water-quality commissions that would require large-scale hog operations to have waste systems that conform to environmental standards.

   1. This would limit the number of hogs that would be allowed on each system to 2,000 head.

   2. The lagoon law would insure that each system wouldn't add any additional poisoning chemicals to the ground water.

C. Finally, the plan would include monitoring and regulating the above codes to insure that each producer is following the rules.

[*Transition*] (Practicality/Cure) This plan will work to reduce nitrate levels in our water supply.

D. The tax breaks and waste-monitoring requirements will result in more, but smaller, swine operations that will do a better job of managing agricultural runoff.

   1. Spreading out the locations of smaller hog farms will lower the concentrations of hogs in any one site.

2. Fewer hogs per farm will make it easier to safely and productively dispose of hog manure.

3. In fact, farmers who raise grain in conjunction with hogs will have the manure right on their land to use as fertilizer for the next year's crop.

E. (Practicality/Cure)The plan will also motivate corporate hog farms to decrease their number of hogs to a more manageable level so they can comply with new water-quality standards.

1. Large-scale hog corporations will be required to prevent nitrates or other dangerous chemicals from infesting our water sources.

2. Operators that do not comply with the regulations set by special water commissions will be penalized for not meeting the standards.

3. Penalties will be severe enough to keep producers trustworthy and to keep the water levels in the United States safe.

F. We know that my plan will work, because Nebraska is using a similar concept with great success.

1. Corporate hog operations are excluded from Nebraska.

2. Water pollution is reduced because hog farms are smaller and distributed over a wider area.

[*Transition*] (Practicality/Advantages vs. Disadvantages) Admittedly, my proposal for hog farming has some potential drawbacks, but these are outweighed by the benefits.

G. The proposed tax breaks for small farmers will need to be funded by state and national governments.

H. Certainly, time and money will be needed to hire employees to monitor and regulate hog numbers and the levels of poisonous compounds.

I. (Counterargument) Some may fear that employment opportunities will be lost if corporate farms cut jobs in response to new water-quality requirements, but this is not likely to be a cost of my proposal.

1. The Missouri Digital News web site reported that agricultural jobs have "actually been declining since the introduction of corporate hog farms," so elimination of corporate farms will probably not add to unemployment.

2. On the other hand, job opportunities might actually increase in rural areas with the creation of many more, smaller hog farms.

3. That has certainly been the case in Nebraska, where the new law has preserved the small family farm and increased job opportunities, while significantly reducing water pollution.

J. Finally, the initial start-up costs of my plan will be more than offset by the increased revenues that will come from cleaner water and a more productive agricultural economy.

    1. Cleaner water will increase recreational opportunities, which, in turn, will generate higher sales taxes.

    2. If drinking-water sources remain clean, cities and municipalities will not have to spend billions of dollars on increasingly sophisticated water-treatment systems.

Conclusion

I. [*Signal end*] I hope you agree with me that high nitrate levels in our water supply is a dangerous problem that needs to be solved.

A. [*Review*] Nitrate poisoning devastates the environment, threatens our drinking water, and attacks the unborn. Fortunately, the plan I have proposed can successfully reduce nitrate levels.

    1. A combination of tax breaks and new water-quality regulations can give some advantages back to small producers who can better control water pollution because they have smaller numbers of animals to manage.

    2. Not only will my plan result in cleaner water, but it will also help preserve the family farm and lead to additional economic benefits to rural regions.

B. When you consider the minimal costs of my plan, keep in mind how much you enjoy your favorite fishing hole.

C. [*Closing Line*] It is up to us to support legislation that will protect life's most precious commodity: clean, safe, refreshing water.

Sample Policy Speech Outline
for analysis and discussion

[Staple]

SPCC 200, [Section]
[Date]

Compact Fluorescent Light Bulbs: A Bright Idea for CSU
By Katelyn Briggs

Specific Purpose Statement: To persuade my audience that Colorado State University should replace all of its incandescent light bulbs with fluorescent light bulbs.

Thesis: I believe that something should be done to save this university's crucial budget money and reduce energy waste here on campus. Today I will argue that 1) though incandescent light bulbs have been used for decades in residential, commercial, and industrial areas, they put off dangerous amounts of heat, waste energy, and are very costly to the consumer. 2) In place of incandescent light bulbs, I propose that we implement the use of compact fluorescent light bulbs because they last longer, provide the same amount of light, produces less heat, use less wattage, and can be safely recycled.

Pattern of Organization: Problem/Solution

Introduction

I. *[Attention Getter]* Half asleep, you stumble into the bathroom, subconsciously reaching for the light switch on the wall.
    A. You get ready to close your eyes, anticipating the bright light to be a familiar rude awakening.
    B. You hit the switch and slowly rub your eyes
    C. But there is no light! You flick the switch back and forth a couple times just to make sure the light is out.
    D. Frustratingly, you think to yourself; didn't I just change this bulb a few months ago?

II. *[Reveal Topic]* I know exactly how that feels because when I step into a bathroom, classroom or hallway at this university, I am thinking the same thing.

III. *[Establish Credibility]* Yes, I change light bulbs at CSU and I see first hand just how much of this universities budget goes to energy bills and light bulbs to keep up with the demand for sufficient lighting at this institution.

IV. *[Thesis and Preview]* I believe that something should be done to save this university's crucial budget money and reduce energy waste here on campus. Today I will argue that:
    A. Though incandescent light bulbs have been used for decades in residential, commercial, and industrial areas, they put off dangerous amounts of heat, waste energy, and are very costly to the consumer.
    B. In place of incandescent light bulbs, I propose that we implement the use of compact fluorescent light bulbs because they last longer, provide the same amount of light, produces less heat, use less wattage, and can be safely recycled.

Body

I. *[Signpost]* First, incandescent light bulbs have been a staple light source for almost a century, so it would be too quick to say that they should be discontinued all together.

    A. According to *Brian Bowers, in his book* <u>Lengthening the Day</u>, electrical lighting and the use of incandescent lights has been tested and used since the mid eighteen hundreds.

    B. According to *Carol Dollard, utilities engineer* here at Colorado State University, incandescent bulbs have an advantage over compact fluorescents because they can be used with dimmer switches for mood lighting during class notes, overheads, and power point projects whereas the compact fluorescent counterparts cannot—yet.

    C. Also, many of today's lamp fixtures are designed specifically for incandescent light bulbs.

        1. In order to fit the compact fluorescent into a base made for an incandescent, *Silicon Valley Power* suggests using an adapter at the end of the base on the compact fluorescent bulb.

[Transition] So, why choose to change out the incandescent lights if they seem so harmless to the university?

    D. (Problem/Need) Well, incandescent light bulbs are not designed around efficiency.

        1. Incandescent bulbs can get extremely hot while in use, reaching temperatures of up to three hundred and fifty degrees Fahrenheit, according to *www.lightsofAmerica.com.*
           a. If the light is not properly covered and is exposed as is the case with many desktop lamps or hanging chandeliers, the bulb and the area around the bulb can get extremely hot and stay hot for a while after the light is no longer in use, making it dangerous for someone to change that bulb.
        2. Also, according to the *Federal Trade Commission: Facts for Consumers* web page, the heat used to create the light coming from an incandescent bulb eats up ninety percent of the energy being used to give light to the consumer.
           a. That means, when the bill comes at the end of the month, you only got ten percent of the light you paid for.
           b. Another problem with this is that in many of the buildings on campus, there is no air conditioning and incandescent light bulbs only create more heat than is absolutely necessary.

II. *[Solution]* (Plan) I propose a plan to implement energy efficient compact fluorescent light bulbs in place of incandescent light bulbs in order to cut back on unnecessary and high-energy costs eating at the budget money our university cannot afford to lose.

    A. (Plan/Cure)First, Colorado State University will see immediate results when using the compact fluorescents.

1. According to *www.howstuffworks.com* these bulbs do not use heat to power the light source coming from the bulb; instead, they use mercury vapor that reacts with electrons to create a stream of light going through a glass tube.
2. This means the bulbs are safe to the touch and will not create extra heat in those stuffy classrooms.
3. Also, without the extra cost of heat, you are not losing wasted energy and you are only paying for the energy used to power the light.

B. (Practicality/Counterargument) But, as I mentioned before, the compact fluorescent bulb does contain a very toxic gas—mercury.
1. Mercury is a necessary component of the fluorescent bulb because it is what reacts with the electrons in the electricity to form the light.
2. This substance has been known to cause birth defects and water contamination when disposed of improperly, where it can leak into the environment or, when heated up, into the air.
3. The solution to this is what outweighs these negative effects—recycling.
    a. According to *Bethlehem Lamp Recycling* web pages, fluorescent lamps can and should be recycled.
    b. There are companies such as *Bethlehem Lamp Recycling* that use large retorts with extreme pressure and heat which recover 99.9 percent of the mercury vapors.
    c. The glass from the lamp is then melted and used again.

C. (Practicality/Advantages vs. Disadvantages) With the use of compact fluorescent bulbs, CSU will see positive repercussions in the years to come.
1. Though compact fluorescents are more expensive per bulb than incandescent bulbs, they last longer.
    a. According to *Carol Dollard,* fluorescent bulbs cost on average six to eight dollars and incandescent bulbs cost fifty cents when the university purchases them.
    b. That seems like a large difference, but according to the *California Energy Commission*, lamps used for the recommended four hours per day, with a lifespan of on average 750 hours per incandescent and 10,000 hours per compact fluorescent, the compact fluorescents last more than ten times longer!
    c. That would also mean you only have to pay to replace each bulb once every six years, whereas the incandescent would have to be replaced about twice per year.
2. Also, the energy the consumer is charged for is measured in watts, which is where compact fluorescents have the advantage.
    a. In my interview with *Carol Dollard,* she stated that an incandescent bulb that is 40 watts is comparable with a compact fluorescent that is 9 watts because extra energy is needed in the wattage of the incandescent to produce the required heat.
    b. That would save you up to 75 percent on future electric bills!

D. To sum up all of these statistics is a visual display taken from the *California Energy Commission Consumer Energy Center* web page of a comparison of incandescent light bulbs to compact fluorescent bulbs for the standard of the two bulbs.

1. As I mentioned before, the wattage is the amount of energy used to power the bulb and these two bulbs, the 100 watt and the 23 watt are interchangeable in a basic incandescent fixture.
2. The lumens that you see up there is the amount of light the bulb puts off, and clearly they both range between 1500-1700 lumens which is barely a noticeable difference in light.
3. The base price for a compact seems steep, but as you can see, one bulb lasts you almost 6 years at the recommended four hours per day.
4. You can see the compact also lasts 10,000 hours compared to not even 1,000 for the incandescent.
5. With all of this in mind and the price to put energy into each bulb, the amount of money saved over three years is pretty tremendous; keeping in mind this is the price to power only one bulb.

Conclusion

III.   [*Signal End*] I hope I have convinced you that it would be beneficial to the university that they change their incandescent bulbs to compact fluorescent bulbs.

A. [*Review*] The budget cuts here at our university need to be addressed, even if in a small way. I believe that this plan will accomplish just that.
   1. Compact fluorescents in place of incandescent bulbs will save money because it uses less wattage and they only need to be changed a fraction of the time an incandescent does because they have a longer life.
   2. Also, compact fluorescents can be recycled, reducing pollutant due to light bulbs, and without the heat factor of the incandescent, compact fluorescents are not extremely hot which makes them safer.

B. When you wonder where the university's money goes and worry about the debt that may bring up your tuition next fall, think of the little things that may help us save money at this university.

C. [*Closing Line*] Energy efficiency is something that is coming into play with not just the university, but the world as a whole and should readily be considered because resources aren't endless and we as humans consume a lot of energy that is waste less and if we look hard enough their may be a very simple solution, starting with light bulbs.

Audience Survey—Policy Speech

Name _____

Topic _____

1. What do you know about this topic?

2. What are your attitudes/opinions on this topic? (for/against/undecided)

3. Do you feel directly affected by this topic? Why/why not?

Policy Speech Work Sheet

Name_____

Topic:

No matter which organizational pattern you choose for your policy speech, there are 3 key issues that any policy speech <u>must</u> prove. This worksheet will help you develop each of those necessary arguments.

Issue 1: Need Prove that there is a need for change and create concern for the problem in your audience's minds.

A. What societal problem will your plan attempt to solve?

B. How significant is this problem?

C. Whom does it affect, and how?

D. How will you get your class audience to care about this problem?

Issue 2: PLAN Outline a clear and practical solution to the problem.

Outline your proposal for change in as much detail as you can foresee. Remember to address such issues as how the plan will be administered, funded, implemented, and enforced.

Issue 3: Practicality Prove that your plan will solve or significantly reduce the problem at hand, and that the advantages of this plan outweigh any potential disadvantages.

Provide specific reasons why your plan will work to solve the problem(s) established in Issue One:

Make a list of the benefits that come from having your plan function the way in which it was designed:

Make a list of the alleged or actual disadvantages of your plan:

Give good reasons why the benefits of your plan outweigh the potential or real disadvantages:

Instructor Comments & Suggestions:

Critique Sheet: Policy Speech

Speaker _____

Topic _____

+ E.
✓ Satisfactory
-- Needs improvement
0 Failed to complete

Specific strengths and areas for improvement:

INTRODUCTION
Gained audience's attention _____
Established credibility _____
Introduced topic clearly _____
Related topic to audience _____
Concise thesis/preview _____

BODY
Main points clear _____
Credible evidence _____
Sufficient evidence _____
Reasoning sound and clear _____
Clear problem (Need) _____
Clear solution (Plan) _____
Plan workable (Practicality) _____
Advantages outweigh
 disadvantages (Practicality) _____
Addressed counterarguments _____
Clear transitions _____
Adapted to audience _____
Pathos _____
Ethos _____

CONCLUSION
Signaled ending of speech _____
Summarized main points _____
Ended with artistic last line _____

DELIVERY
Maintained eye contact _____
Used vocal variety _____
Projected adequately _____
Pronunciation correct _____
Articulation clear _____
Rate appropriate _____
Paused effectively _____
Gestures purposeful _____
Mannerisms appropriate _____
Facial expression _____
Extemporaneous style _____
Effective speaking notes _____

Q&A
Listened carefully to questions _____
Managed session well _____
Answered questions clearly
 and effectively _____

VISUAL AIDS
Clear & easy to see   _____
Professionally designed   _____
Aesthetically appealing   _____
Visual, rather than verbal   _____
Incorporated well into the
  speech   _____
Technology used
 appropriately   _____

OUTLINE
Complete sentence format   _____
Logical subordination   _____
Labels included   _____
Works cited page   _____
Spelling accurate   _____
Grammatically correct   _____
Free of typographical errors _____

OVERALL EVALUATON
Topic challenging/appropriate   _____
Completed in time limit   _____

Instructor comments and suggestions:

TIME _____

SCORE _____/250

Listening Sheet: Policy Speech
Research

Listener:

Speaker: Topic:

During the speech, record the speaker's source citations and types of supporting material. Then, reflect on the quality of the research as it related to development of the speaker's arguments.

Front page: complete during the speech
Sources:

<u>Citation</u>   <u>Type of Research</u>

Back page: complete after the speech is done
Did the speaker cite sources clearly throughout the speech?

Which main points were particularly well supported with research?

Which main points would have benefited from more support?

Which source citation(s) contributed most to the speaker's credibility? Why?

Which source citation(s) helped the speaker adapt to her/his class audience? Why?

What could the speaker have done differently with his/her sources to improve speaker credibility and audience adaptation?

Listening Sheet: Policy Speech
Policy Issues

Listener:

Speaker: Topic:

During the speech, record the speaker's claims and corresponding evidence for each of the 3 key policy issues. Then, evaluate the quality of the speaker's policy arguments.

Front page: complete during the speech
Need
Claim(s)   Evidence

Plan
Claim(s)   Evidence

Practicality
 Claim(s)   Evidence

Back page: complete after the speech is done

What counterarguments to this policy can you think of that the speaker either failed to address or failed to disprove sufficiently?

What suggestions can you provide this speaker for strengthening his/her audience appeal?

**Listening Sheet: Policy Speech
Delivery**

Listener:

Speaker: Topic:

Identify 2 of the speaker's delivery *strengths* (comment on volume, pitch, rate, pauses, vocal variety, pronunciation, articulation, dialect, appearance, bodily action, gestures, and eye contact).

Identify 2 *areas for improvement* in the speaker's delivery (comment on volume, pitch, rate, pauses, vocal variety, pronunciation, articulation, dialect, appearance, bodily action, gestures, and eye contact).

What speech preparation or practice techniques would you recommend to the speaker to improve her/his delivery?

UNIT SIX: COMMEMORATIVE SPEAKING

📄 **Reading:** *Invitation to Public Speaking*, Ch. 19 & review Ch. 12

Unit Objectives: Upon completion of this unit, you should be able to:

✓ identify the different types of speeches delivered on special occasions

✓ understand the connection between commemoration and community values

✓ use language to make your speech appealing and memorable

✓ deliver a commemorative speech from manuscript

Assignment: Commemorative Speech

Prepare and present a 4-5 minute speech that pays tribute to a person, concept, organization, or institution. This speech will be delivered from manuscript. Organize your speech's main points according to those virtues exhibited by the subject you have chosen to amplify. Incorporate examples of both imagery and rhythm into your speech, and label them on your manuscript. Prior to the delivery, submit 2 copies of your manuscript. It should be computer-printed (or typed), double-spaced, and conform to standards of good writing and spelling, typographical, or grammatical errors.

The Commemorative Speech Assignment Emphasizes the Following Skills:

⇨ Communication & Community Values: Identify and illustrate the virtues possessed by your subject.

⇨ Language: Choose each word carefully and employ colorful, concrete, and evocative language.

⇨ Delivery: Have a fully-polished delivery that employs dramatic pauses, vocal variations, and phrasing. Because there is no research required for this speech, you are expected to extra time into practicing your delivery.

☑ **Tips & Suggestions: Preparing Your Commemorative Speech**
By Carl R. Burgchardt, Ph.D.

The Commemorative Speech combines elements of informative and persuasive speaking; however, it is unlike previous assignments. It contains information about your subject, but it must go beyond simple biography to inspire your audience. In other words, the Commemorative Speech will be more than an encyclopedia entry that merely lists the historical facts of a person, concept, organization, thing, or institution. The purpose of the speech is to arouse and heighten admiration for your subject. You should try to penetrate to the essence of your topic, to generate a deep sense of appreciation and respect for the object of your praise. The assignment contains elements of persuasive speaking in that you are attempting to convince your audience that your subject is praiseworthy. Unlike deliberative speaking, however, the Commemorative Speech does not make explicit arguments, *per se*. Instead, the speech of tribute proceeds by *amplifying* the praiseworthy attributes of your subject. You must illustrate the positive virtues of your topic—things like honor, courage, compassion, faithfulness, and so forth.

In developing the virtues of your subject, it is important to *show, not simply tell*. In other words, you must use concrete, vivid language that illustrates and amplifies the virtues possessed by your subject. A person could simply assert "My mother was unselfish." But the point is made much more vividly and convincingly by relaying an anecdote: "Many a night my mother never set a place for herself at the dinner table. She always told us kids that she had eaten at work. We never understood until much later that she went to bed hungry so that we had enough to eat." In the first instance, the speaker merely asserts a generalization; in the second example, the speaker illustrates in a dramatic fashion that the subject possesses a widely praised virtue.

Topic Selection

In selecting a topic for this assignment, be certain that the subject of your speech is indeed praiseworthy. In order for a human action to be considered praiseworthy, it must be *intentional* and *your audience must perceive it as virtuous*. For instance, a clumsy person might accidentally trip over a curb and inadvertently push a small child out of the path of a bus. While the effect of this action was to save the life of a child, the intent of the clumsy person was not courageous, so the behavior of the clumsy person is not really praiseworthy. In addition, a tragedy may happen to an individual that profoundly alters his or her life. For example, the subject of your speech may have developed cancer. Remember to praise the virtuous *reaction* to the tragedy and not the tragedy itself. In other words, don't praise a person for developing cancer; rather, praise the subject's heroic or dignified or wise reaction to the disease. We praise *intentional actions*, not accidents or misfortunes in themselves. Of course, if the subject of your speech is not human, then the question of intention is not really relevant.

Secondly, be certain that your audience will consider the behavior or attribute of your subject to be praiseworthy. No doubt, at the national convention of the Hell's Angels motorcycle gang, the ability to drink profusely might be considered a virtue. In that context, with that particular audience, a speaker might praise a fellow gang member for being a heavy drinker. But, in the general public, the ability to consume massive quantities of alcohol is not usually considered a virtue—quite the opposite. In another example, suppose a speaker wanted to praise rap music. Younger audiences may relish the driving beat and provocative lyrics of rap music, while older audiences may be offended by the social commentary and alienated by the lack of melody. Depending upon the composition of your audience, provocative lyrics may or may not be a praiseworthy attribute. In sum, then, before selecting a subject, be sure that your audience will share your sense of what is admirable. You must praise your subject in terms of the values your audience embraces.

In general, you should select a subject with which you are personally familiar and about which you care. There are two reasons for this. First, it is easier to invent appropriate materials for your subject if you already know all about it, and it will save you from having to do library research. Second, if you truly care about a subject, your personal conviction will shine through in the stylistic choices you make and in the quality of your delivery. If you are filled with genuine emotion, your speech will be enlivened by it.

Most students probably should select a person to praise. Parents, grandparents, siblings, spouses, "significant others," children, aunts and uncles, are natural and appropriate choices. You might also select a favorite teacher, coach, neighbor, minister, and the like. The more specific, familiar, and sincere your choice is, the better.

While it is more difficult, you also might choose objects or places like Rocky Mountain National Park, Old Town, the Trolley, the Poudre River, Moby Arena, the Oval, and so forth. These topics are more abstract, but it is still possible to praise them according to widely-accepted virtues. You also could praise organizations, events, or institutions, such as United Way, the Boy Scouts, Colorado State University, the Fort Collins Symphony, the Bolder Boulder race, CSU Rams football games, and so on.

Abstract concepts are the most challenging topics, but it is theoretically possible to praise general ideas such as democracy, nature, freedom, meditation, art, music, or dance. However, students should be cautious about selecting such a subject: the more abstract the topic, the more difficult it is to invent and amplify virtues through the use of concrete language and specific stylistic devices. For the most part, we will assume that you will give a speech of tribute about people. Over the years, these have been the most consistently successful topics. *If you select another sort of topic, be certain to discuss this choice with your instructor well before your speech is due.*

Development and Organization

How does one invent and arrange materials for this speech? Unlike the informative and persuasive speeches, there are no sure-fire formats or structures for organizing the Commemorative Speech. However, there are some criteria or general principles that you may use to guide your efforts. First, it is a mistake to try to force your subject into a pre-established formula or to begin with preconceived ideas. On the other hand, it is an error to stare at a blank piece of paper or computer screen and hope for inspiration from above. The best way to invent appropriate materials for this speech is the Stream-of-Consciousness Method. To do this, go to a quiet place where you can get into a contemplative mood. Then, meditate upon your subject. Immerse yourself in memories; read old letters; view photographs; fill yourself with warm, uplifting thoughts. When a positive memory occurs to you, write down the gist of it on an index card. At this point, don't be analytical or evaluative; just get it down on index cards. Concentrate on visual imagery, fragrances, bits of conversation, typical quotations, familiar activities, and the like. Allow the memories to pour out of you. The only discipline you must follow is to put each discrete impression or memory on a separate index card. This will make it easier to organize the speech later.

Some students are not comfortable giving a speech on a personal subject. In that case, it is perfectly fine to give a speech of tribute about a person or thing of national or international importance, from the past or present. Examples of appropriate subjects might be Martin Luther King, Mother Teresa, Albert Schweitzer, Susan B. Anthony, Wrigley Field, the Empire State Building, Niagara Falls, the Golden Gate Bridge, and so forth. Obviously, this sort of speech will require research, but the same inventional process that one uses for a personal topic still applies here. You must immerse yourself in the particulars of your subject's life or history. Surround yourself with biographies, autobiographies, diaries, letters and writings, photographs, audio and visual recordings, and other relevant materials. Allow these images, quotations, concepts, feelings, to fill up your mind and senses. Then, following the Stream-of-Consciousness Method, write down discreet impressions on separate index cards in the same fashion as if you were doing a personal topic.

When you have accumulated a substantial stack of cards, try to sort them out into psychologically-related themes or topics. Ask yourself, what does this bit of memory illustrate about my subject? For example, you might remember the smell of chocolate chip cookies baking in your mother's kitchen and associate this fragrance with a feeling of affection or devotion:

> Whenever I smell the delicious aroma of chocolate chip cookies baking in the oven, for a moment I become a small child again, sitting in my mother's kitchen. My mom knew how much I loved chocolate chip cookies. On special winter afternoons, just the two of us would make up a batch and feast on the gooey confections, hot from the oven. Love comes in many shapes and forms. For me, one kind of love smells like chocolate chip cookies, baking in the oven.

This quotation is merely one example of how you might translate a discreet memory into an illustration of a virtue. And, importantly, it is an illustration with which many in your audience will be able to relate. The use of concrete, descriptive language allows your audience to "experience" the memory and share your appreciation of it.

As you move through your stack of cards, sort the illustrations into separate themes or categories of virtues, such as love, intelligence, compassion, dignity, energy, sense of humor, integrity, and the like. As your categories emerge, you may do some shifting of cards to better illustrate and amplify the main themes of your speech. Some categories will be underdeveloped; others will be extensive. At this point, don't edit or be overly critical. Simply arrange the cards into piles and try to make each pile thematically unified. The only rule is, each stack of cards will illustrate, that is, *show*, not simply tell, a value or virtue that the audience is likely to accept.

Now, make a rough draft out of these stacks of index cards. Each pile will be converted into one or more paragraphs that illustrate a virtue. This is still early in the process, so don't worry about redundancy, choppiness, or stylistic quality. Just express your thoughts in sentences, taking care to expand upon every feeling and insight. When you are finished with this draft, you should have a series of paragraphs. Each paragraph should *illustrate* a virtue. Your rough draft can be compared to the stanzas of a prose poem. Each paragraph or "stanza" establishes and amplifies a distinctive virtue.

The next stage is to work on the internal development of each paragraph. Refine the progression of quotations, imagery, and description, so that one idea builds on another in a psychologically-compelling way. Think about building suspense or a sense of mystery or wonder as each paragraph unfolds. Work on the unity and cohesiveness of individual paragraphs. Unity means that a paragraph is devoted to one theme. Cohesiveness means that all of the sentences in the paragraph "hold together" in an ordered, consistent way.

Take a pencil or marker and begin striking out redundancies and awkward sentences. Clarify ambiguities; work on internal transitions that link sentences; add material to complete ideas. At this point, begin to consciously refine or introduce metaphors, similes, imagery. Enhance the natural rhythms of your prose by introducing or bolstering parallelism, repetition, and alliteration. These things may already be latent in your rough draft. Your job now is to bring them out and polish them. As you complete your revisions, you should be able to explain the position and function of each word, phrase, and sentence in the paragraph.

This is also the stage where you need to write an appropriate introduction and conclusion for your speech. Like any address, you must plan your introduction, body, and conclusion. In general, the introduction sets the mood, develops audience expectations, introduces the subject, and *subtly* announces the structure. You would *not* say: "Today I am going to argue that my mother is a wonderful person. I have three main arguments to support this claim: (1) she is compassionate; (2) she is brave; (3) she is imaginative." You *might* say something like:

> Compassion, courage, creativity—these three words are easy to say, but difficult to exemplify. They form a code, a plan of living that extraordinary people try to emulate. One such extraordinary person is my mother, Emily Ann Brown. If she had a motto, it would be "Compassion, courage, creativity."

Once you have completed the introduction, the body of the speech should be composed of three to six unified and cohesive paragraphs that establish and amplify the virtues of your subject. The conclusion restates and synthesizes the values of the speech. It also provides a *truly* memorable ending line, often returning to a concept or quotation used in the introduction. In the hypothetical example we have been using, the speech might well end with the words "Compassion, courage, creativity."

No one structure or plan is ideal for the Commemorative Speech. Select an organizational scheme that matches you and your subject. Don't be afraid to use the devices of drama and suspense. For example, in one memorable speech, a student began her speech with a vivid description of a funeral. The speaker figuratively brought this scene before the eyes of the audience. She explained that hundreds of people were gathered for the funeral of a high school principal. During the course of the funeral, the speaker described her thoughts and memories of this outstanding educator. At the very end of the speech, the student revealed that the high school principal was her father. This revelation, which came as a total surprise to the audience, brought all of the speaker's remarks into startling focus and resulted in a poignant moment. The use of a surprising revelation at the end of a speech can be highly effective, but don't abuse this technique. Another student told a tale of how he lost his "best friend." After waxing nostalgic about all of the wonderful adventures he shared with his friend, he related the fateful day when his playmate fell from the top of the jungle gym and was killed instantly. In the last line of the speech, the speaker revealed that his best friend was a hamster! Although the loss of a pet is a sad thing, this student cynically manipulated the audience, and the reaction of his classmates was dismay and anger.

As the above examples indicate, time and place do not have to be treated in a strictly chronological way; indeed, the Commemorative Speech is often stronger if it does not follow a conventional, informative pattern. A better course is to select a structure that allows you to focus on virtues rather than a dull narrative that recounts "this happened, then that happened, then this happened." A speech may begin with the end of a person's life or entail flashbacks; it may begin with a characteristic saying, pose, place, or feeling. It may end in the same ways. The goal is to *show* to the audience the virtues of your subject, not to convey abstract or mundane details about birth, childhood, education, career, retirement, etc.

Delivery

Unlike the other speeches of the semester, this assignment will be read from manuscript. That means you will deliver the speech exactly as it is written. Since this is a manuscript speech, there is no excuse for falling outside of the time limits. Therefore, when you have finished polishing and editing your speech, you will need to time it exactly. Cut or expand the speech to fit precisely between 4 and 5 minutes. Then, produce a clean manuscript to hand in to your instructor. This should be double-spaced and be free of typos, and spelling, grammar, and punctuation errors. Remember to hand in two copies of your speech, as you have done with previous assignments. A substantial part of your grade will be based on the quality of the manuscript you submit.

Once you have accomplished these tasks, prepare a reading copy of your manuscript—the one you will use to deliver the speech. The reading copy should be marked up with underlining and instructions on pauses, intonations, volume, and so forth. The reading copy may be typed triple-spaced or printed in oversized type. That is up to you. Many students find it helpful to glue their sheets of paper to stiff cardboard for ease of handling, or to encase the manuscript in "slick sheets"—hole-punched, plastic sheaths that can be inserted into a notebook. In any event, prepare your manuscript in a way that will allow you maximum ease and freedom when delivering your speech. You should be able to hold your manuscript with one hand, leaving the other hand free for page turning or gesturing.

To be successful, you must practice reading your speech aloud on many occasions. You should rehearse the speech until it is nearly memorized (or actually memorized). Above all, on the day of the speech, you must avoid the impression that you are reading your manuscript for the first time. You should be so familiar with your manuscript, that once you begin a sentence or a line of text, you can finish it without looking at it. As you are delivering your speech, try to maintain good eye contact with the audience. You want to *sound* spontaneous and sincere, even though every word has been carefully planned and rehearsed. Reliance on the manuscript is analogous to the way a train keeps on the tracks. The train has great momentum, and will keep moving whether it is on the tracks or not. The tracks simply guide the force of the train. So too, the lines of the manuscript are the "tracks" that keep your speech moving forward in a precise direction. Finally, think of this speech as a performance. Delivery of the Commemorative Speech is more akin to acting than to ordinary speech delivery. You should use dramatic pauses; vary the tone of your voice; vary the volume and rate; and use gestures and facial expressions to underscore the meaning of the words.

The best way to approach this assignment is to give a sincere speech from your heart. If you conscientiously attempt to use the stylistic devices discussed in your textbook, and if you practice, the chances are good that you will surprise yourself and your classmates, and you will deliver the most eloquent speech of your life. Moreover, students in the past have used this assignment as an opportunity to express exactly how they feel about special people in their lives. Parents, spouses, relatives, children, grandparents, coaches, special teachers, friends, would all be deeply moved if they received a copy of your manuscript as a gift. Or, if the subject of your speech is deceased, this is an excellent opportunity to create a lasting tribute that friends and relatives would cherish. Sometimes, these speeches are actually given outside of class. One student was expected to make a speech at her parents' twenty-fifth wedding anniversary, and she used this assignment to develop the oration. Her family was truly moved by the smoothness of her delivery and the eloquence of her language.

Sometimes students feel that they don't know anyone famous or heroic or successful enough to praise publicly in a speech. They are embarrassed that their subject is not wealthy or powerful. But, as we all know, seemingly ordinary individuals often lead extraordinary lives, but they do it quietly and privately. Hard work, dignity, integrity, love of life are wonderful virtues that are exhibited every day by people who may not be "successful" by materialistic standards. The following model speech is an example of how you might go about praising so-called "ordinary" people.

Commemorative Speech: Manuscript for Analysis

Note on labeling stylistic devices: In this manuscript, subscript is used to label stylistic devices. Your instructor may prefer that you underline or highlight stylistic devices and write in labels by hand. Use whatever method your instructor advises and allows for accuracy and clarity.

Lina

By Katherine Gould

(Paragraph develops an extended tree metaphor and employs parallelism) Like a quivering Aspen (simile) she stood; with her roots firmly planted in the soil of wisdom (metaphor), with her trunk steadfast and strong against the ferocious winds of time (metaphor), with her branches offered to the world that sought to cut her down an embrace of compassion (metaphor), and with her leaves spread toward the sun in reverence for the giver of life. She stood. I speak to you not of a famous woman, but of a woman who was a friend, a minister, a mother—my mother, Lina (antithesis). She was a friend whose wisdom aided those in need, a minister whose strength kept her going against enormous odds, and a mother whose compassion and reverence influenced her child to look at life and the people in it as caring and beautiful (parallelism).

While I know I shall always remember moments with my mother, like the times when we read the *Little House on the Prairie* collection and Greek mythology as bedtime stories, or the times she played soccer with me to help me practice for a big game, I know I will remember her mostly for the conversations we had. She was wise. During these times she passed on knowledge about her life, mistakes she made, and the wisdom she had learned along the way. She talked to me as an equal. She talked to me as someone who had a valid viewpoint always worth hearing and considering, and she talked to me in order to push me to make me think harder (repetition "she talked"). She was always bringing up topics that others might have thought to be too difficult. She spoke of politics, sex, depression, and yes—even death. She pushed me to learn more and ask questions. There is one such conversation that stands out more than any other. A conversation that showed her wisdom.

Picture a young single mother sitting at the kitchen table with a bowl full of cherries and her five-year old daughter. Try to imagine the wisdom and strength it took for this woman to tell her daughter that she had breast cancer, that she was sick, that she could die (parallelism), and that she might not be around in the near future. My mother was wise. She told me what to expect: from hospital trips and doctor visits, to the possible best and worst of the situation, to the expected and the unknown. She helped me to understand so that I wouldn't be afraid of what lay ahead. The rest of that year and continuing on into the next was hard, but my mother remained strong.

Through the years that followed my mother's battle with cancer only became fiercer. After her first experience with cancer we crossed our fingers and waited to see if she was out of the clear. One month, two months, six months, a year (parallelism), time passed and cancer's memory was fading fast until my mother went for a check up and once again a lump was found. But unlike the first time, when the doctors had been able to remove all the cancer through surgery and chemotherapy, this time they took her breast as well. It was part of what defined her as a woman, and it took all her strength to remain standing strong and appear whole. She had other responsibilities to think about—fulfilling her role as a minister and counselor, friend and confidant, mother and teacher (parallelism). It took tremendous strength to deal with this. She did not dwell, did not crumble under pressure. She stood. Strong and tall, ready to move onto the challenges that were yet to come.

Time passed again. This time we hoped but were less naïve. This time cancer's memory did not fade. This time we had to face the ordeals that my mother would endure. She took what she had learned and the strength she had gained and opened her arms and heart to the world. Through these trials and tribulations she grew more compassionate and more reverent. Before her bouts with cancer, my mother gave sermons every Sunday, headed committees and made visits, but after the second battle with cancer she undertook a more important role. She became the rock that people leaned on (metaphor). I remember evenings where we would receive a call from someone in need of a shoulder to cry on and she would spend the next three hours talking to them. My mother's door was open to anyone; even people outside her parish would visit because they had heard she could help.

As wise, strong, and compassionate as she was, her time was coming to an end. During the summer before I was to start my sixth grade year, she once again was diagnosed with cancer; however, this time it had spread to her bones. Her x-rays were pictures of dark, demented, disturbing (alliteration) shadows that were haunting (metaphor) my mother's body. The only hope lay in a bone marrow transplant, but her life was not meant to continue. During the transplant process, my mother contracted pneumonia and was placed on a respirator. This action later lead to complications and on May 3, 1994 she died. Her tree no longer stands, her roots are no longer there, her trunk no longer withstands the winds of time, her branches no longer embrace the world and her leaves have fallen. She was my mother, Lina (concluding lines return to the extended metaphor, employing imagery and mirroring the introduction. They also use parallel structure).

Topic Proposal: Commemorative Speech

Name:_____

Propose two potential topics for your Commemorative Speech. List them below, in order of preference, and explain why you think your subjects are praiseworthy.

Topic 1:

List 2-3 virtues exemplified by your subject, and briefly note the anecdotes or examples you will use to illustrate each virtue.

Topic 2:

List 2-3 virtues exemplified by your subject, and briefly note the anecdotes or examples you will use to illustrate each virtue.

Instructor Comments: Topic 1 _____Approved _____Not Approved
                                Topic 2 _____Approved _____Not Approved

Listening Sheet: Commemorative Speech
Commemoration and Community Values

Listener:

Speaker: Topic:

Identify the virtues the speaker chose to illustrate, and the examples/descriptions used to amplify them. Then, reflect upon how well the speaker tapped into community values in this speech.

Front page: complete during the speech
<u>Virtue</u>   <u>Example</u>

Back page: complete after the speech is done
Was the speaker's choice of virtues well-adapted to the class audience & the assignment? Why or why not?

What suggestions can you give to the speaker for improving the amplification of virtues in this speech?

What have you learned from the commemorative speaking round about the relationship between emotional appeal in speeches and community values?

Listening Sheet: Commemorative Speech
Style & Language

Listener:

Speaker: Topic:

Identify examples of imagery and rhythm in the speech. Then, reflect on how the speaker's language choices enhanced or detracted from the speech.

Front page: complete during the speech
As you hear them in the speech, write down examples of the following stylistic devices:

Concrete words:

Metaphor:

Simile:

Personification

Alliteration:

Parallelism:

Repetition:

Antithesis:

Back page: complete after the speech is done
What imagery device was most effective in this speech, and why?

How could the speaker have used imagery and/or rhythm differently to improve his/her speech?

Comment on the speaker's delivery. Did the speaker use vocal variety, pauses, eye contact, etc. to maximize the effectiveness of her/his language choices?

**Listening Sheet: Commemorative Speech
Delivery**

Listener:

Speaker: Topic:

Identify 2 of the speaker's delivery *strengths* (comment on volume, pitch, rate, pauses, vocal variety, pronunciation, articulation, dialect, appearance, bodily action, gestures, and eye contact).

Identify 2 *areas for improvement* in the speaker's delivery (comment on volume, pitch, rate, pauses, vocal variety, pronunciation, articulation, dialect, appearance, bodily action, gestures, and eye contact).

What speech preparation or practice techniques would you recommend to the speaker to improve her/his delivery?

Self-Evaluation Sheet: Commemorative Speech

Name:_____Topic:_____

1. What do you feel were the major strengths of your speech?
   (comment on organization, delivery, and use of linguistic devices)

2. How have your speech composition and delivery skills improved over the course of the semester?

3. Give an example of how/where/when you might use this type of speech in your future.

4. What information or skills will you take away from this class for use in future personal or professional contexts?

5. How has your nervousness improved throughout the semester?